ALSO BY KATHLEEN McGOWAN

The Expected One

The Book of Love

The
SOURCE
of
MIRACLES

7 Steps to Transforming Your Life
Through the Lord's Prayer

KATHLEEN McGOWAN

A FIRESIDE BOOK
Published by Simon & Schuster

New York   London   Toronto   Sydney

Fireside
A Division of Simon & Schuster, Inc.
1230 Avenue of the Americas
New York, NY 10020

First Fireside hardcover edition November 2009

FIRESIDE and colophon are registered trademarks of Simon & Schuster, Inc.

For information about special discounts for bulk purchases,
please contact Simon & Schuster Special Sales at 1-866-506-1949
or business@simonandschuster.com.

The Simon & Schuster Speakers Bureau can bring authors to your live event.
For more information or to book an event contact the Simon & Schuster
Speakers Bureau at 1-866-248-3049 or visit our website at www.simonspeakers.com.

Designed by Ruth Lee-Mui

Manufactured in the United States of America

1   3   5   7   9   10   8   6   4   2

Library of Congress Cataloging-in-Publication Data

McGowan, Kathleen.
The source of miracles : 7 steps to transforming your life
through the Lord's prayer / by Kathleen McGowan.
p.   cm.
1. Lord's prayer.   2. Spirtual life.   3. Miracles.   I. Title.
BV230.M2519   2009
226.9'606—dc22   2009007023

ISBN 978-1-4391-3765-9
ISBN 978-1-4391-4954-6 (ebook)

For Shane

Our Father in Heaven,
May Your Name Be Hallowed,
May Your Kingdom Come,
May Your Will Be Done,
As in Heaven, So upon Earth.
Give Us Today Our Sufficient Bread,
And Forgive Us Our Debts,
As We Also Have Forgiven Our Debtors.
And Do Not Bring Us into Temptation,
But Deliver Us from Evil.

This version of the Lord's Prayer comes from a literal translation of the New Testament by the late scholar Richmond Lattimore. I have chosen to use this translation as I believe it is the closest we can come to the words that Jesus spoke in the Gospel of Matthew, chapter 6, verses 9–13, based upon original texts in the Greek. It is similar to the most commonly read English translation, the New International Version. Please see the appendixes for alternate versions and for an explanation on the doxology, "For thine is the kingdom and the power and the glory."

THE ROSE WITH SIX PETALS:

A Treasure Map to the Source of Miracles

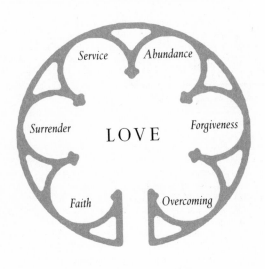

Contents

XI

The Center of the Rose—Love

XII

Final Thoughts: What Would Jesus Do?

APPENDIXES

Which Version of the Lord's Prayer Do You Prefer?

Inspirational Prayers to Supplement Your Practice

Acknowledgments

I

Introduction—The Lord's Prayer

On Easter Sunday in the year 2007, the *Los Angeles Times* reported that two billion people worldwide were united by one powerful common denominator: the Lord's Prayer. On that date, nearly *one third of the planet's population* recited that prayer in their native languages as an expression of faith.

While Christianity has been divided since its inception into factions with theological differences, this single prayer unifies all of them. The content of the Lord's Prayer cannot be affected by dogma or politics. Even while different denominations may make minor variations, the essential words and the teachings they impart remain unchanged since the day that Jesus first taught them to his followers. The two billion souls who call themselves Christians often differ in more ways than they are alike, yet this single prayer is the common ground for all of them. Jesus gave us a prayer so universal and impactful that it would endure for thousands of years and against the harshest odds. It is not only indelible, it is eternal.

The Lord's Prayer is now, as it was when Jesus lived, the incorruptible formula for personal and global transformation.

Most Christians learn the Lord's Prayer in early childhood and can recite it by rote and without effort. It is so ingrained in our memories that we don't even have to think about it.

And therein lies the problem. *We don't even have to think about it.*

While most of us can rattle off this greatest of prayers and know that it is a cornerstone of Christianity, the full extent of our understanding often ends right about there. Many of us have forgotten the extraordinary power and meaning behind the words, if we ever thought about them to begin with. I learned the Lord's Prayer when I was three years old, in preschool, many years before I would ever know what words like *hallowed*, *trespasses*, or *temptation* meant. There wasn't a child in my class who could have told you the meaning behind the prayer, and yet we were all able to recite it flawlessly on Parents' Night. We were taught to speak it on cue, like obedient little parrots who could make the appropriate sounds come out after endless repetitions but had no ability to understand the somewhat exotic-sounding syllables.

I can assure you that we were not taught the origins of the prayer as children, and even if someone had tried to explain it to us, we were far too young to understand it as a dynamic spiritual practice and a foolproof recipe for creating a joyous and fulfilled life.

So we grow up never knowing that, with the Lord's Prayer, Jesus was giving us the formula for manifesting miracles—not only when we most need them, but on a very regular basis.

While interviewing a random selection of Christians from different denominations, I was stunned to find how few of them even knew that this prayer came directly from Jesus. "Wait a minute—*Jesus* created the Lord's Prayer?" was the shocked question I heard over and over again. Even some truly devout churchgoers looked at me in surprise when I said this prayer was the work of Jesus. Some didn't believe me, even when I cited the gospel accounts that attest to this origin. One replied, "But they didn't teach us that in school," as if such an omission in our spiritual education were unusual!

But Jesus was, in fact, the author of this most perfectly constructed blueprint for spiritual change. In the New Testament, the Lord's Prayer can be found in the Gospel of Matthew in chapter 6, verses 9–13, as a component of his Sermon on the Mount, and then again in Luke, chapter 11, verses 1–4, when one of the disciples asks Jesus to "teach us to pray." And teach us he did. In doing so, he gave us this priceless treasure: a set of simple and unchangeable directions, in the form of a prayer, for discovering the real secret of how to have the life you truly desire: a life filled with love, happiness, and yes, even wealth. The prayer shows us that all these wonderful gifts come about through an increase in faith: faith in God, faith in ourselves, and faith in our fellow humans—in that order.

The Lord's Prayer addresses the issues that hurt us, confound us, and impede our progress, and illuminates the way in which we can overcome these obstacles. The prayer is our guide to purifying our spirit of anything that troubles it and holds us back from being "fully realized" human beings—which is to say, human beings functioning at our highest potential, a potential that leads directly to happiness and abundance. Using this prayer regularly as a spiritual practice creates real and lasting change at the soul level, change which becomes manifest in very earthly, visible ways.

When spoken with faith and intention, these are literally magic words.

On the eve of my thirtieth birthday in the spring of 1993, I became an ordained minister as an expression of my commitment to studying and understanding the teachings of Jesus. Fifteen years, thousands of pages of reading, and hundreds of hours of spirited discussions later, I have come to what some may consider a simplistic, and therefore perhaps controversial, view of Christian teachings. I believe that if you study and hold tight to the Lord's Prayer, the Beatitudes, a handful of parables, and what Jesus tells us in Matthew 22, verses 37–39—*love the Lord thy God with all thy heart and love thy neighbor as thyself*—then you pretty much have everything you need to live a perfect life and encourage peace on earth. But foremost of these gifts, the center from which all blessings spring, is the Lord's Prayer. While the other elements teach us valuable spiritual lessons, this great prayer is the tool that connects us immediately and directly to the source that is within each of us: the source of faith, the source of love, the source of forgiveness. And in combination, those things are the source of very real miracles.

My own life has been transformed dramatically by utilizing the Lord's Prayer as a regular spiritual practice. As a result, I have witnessed the most miraculous events, including wonders of life and death. I have been blessed with extraordinary abundance and joy. But this was not always the case.

To show you how I came to truly know the Lord's Prayer as the perfect formula for dramatic transformation—and how you can do the same—I must first take you with me into the past, through the once locked doors of a secret society and into the heart of a medieval mystery school.

I must first introduce you to the Mystery of the Rose with Six Petals.

II

The Mystery of the Rose with Six Petals

LOS ANGELES: AUGUST 17, 2001

Our beautiful baby boy would be dead within an hour.

That's what the doctors said. And had I believed them, he likely would have died exactly as they predicted. But I didn't believe them, and I didn't because of what I learned from the rose with six petals.

The youngest of our three sons, Shane Francis, was born on an August afternoon in 2001, perfect and healthy. Or so we thought. He appeared to be having a little trouble breathing after a few hours into his life here on earth, but we were told that this was not uncommon with a baby born via cesarean section. At this stage, no one was too worried. He was placed under an oxygen tent and observed in the nursery for a few hours.

And then he turned blue—before turning an ashen shade of ghastly gray. He was no longer able to breathe on his own. His lungs simply ceased to function. We would discover later that he had been born with a deadly condition that made it impossible for his lungs to inflate.

But this wasn't even necessarily the most immediate concern. The crisis came from the realization that he had essentially been deprived of oxygen for several hours before anyone realized it. There was, at this stage, permanent damage to his newborn organs, including his brain.

While the suburban hospital Shane was born in had a neonatal intensive care unit (NICU), they were not optimistic about his chances of survival when he was transferred into their ward. He did not respond to any of the respirators he was hooked up to; it was simply too late to save him.

The NICU doctors thought I was in an understandable state of maternal denial when I told them they were wrong. As a result, a mild-mannered social worker from the hospital was sent to "counsel us." In other words, his job was to make sure we understood that our baby was about to die.

"This isn't your fault," the well-intentioned man assured me as he patted me on the back. "You didn't do anything to cause this. It's just one of those things that we can't foresee. But if you have a priest, minister, or other spiritual adviser, I suggest you call him or her now to help you get through this. There are only a few minutes of life left in this baby."

I knew that he meant well, but I really just wanted him to shut up. I was furious that they had all given up on my baby, that they were taking the position that he was already dead, when he was still alive in the same room with us.

But I also knew something they didn't know. I knew that my baby would live, no matter what they said, because I had seen it while praying in the center of a labyrinth three months earlier. I had, in fact, caught my first glimpse of the miracles that were to follow a full six years earlier, over six thousand miles away in a cathedral in France.

CHARTRES, FRANCE: MAY 1995

There is a legend that when Napoleon stormed through the doors of the Cathedral of Notre Dame de Chartres for the first time, the glory of the place stopped him in his tracks. He grew very silent—a rarity— as he looked around, taking in the majesty, the artistry, and the sanctity. In a choked voice he announced to his entourage, "Chartres is no place for an atheist."

I beg to differ. I think that Chartres is a perfect place for an atheist. The glory and grace of the structure have the potential to convince even the most hardened skeptic of the presence of God. If ever there was a monument that was divinely guided and inspired to illustrate the concept of "on earth as it is in heaven," it is Chartres Cathedral.

I had my first look at Chartres from approximately twenty miles away while driving through France, "coincidentally" on Mother's Day in 1995. The mismatched yet magnificent spires pointed to heaven from their place on a hilltop that has been sacred to mankind for thousands of years. To describe the majesty of Chartres in detail is beyond the scope of this book; it just may be beyond my ability to ever find the right words to do it justice. Orson Welles, who knew a few things about genius, said Chartres Cathedral was "the premier work of mankind . . . a celebration of God's glory and the dignity of man." I find his description perfectly fitting now that I have seen the miracles that emerge from such a place.

But in May of 1995, I was a tourist more than I was a pilgrim. To call myself a pilgrim would indicate that I knew how sacred and special the place was when I set out to visit it. I did not. While I knew that the cathedral was a heritage site for its glorious eight-hundred-year-old architecture and hundreds of magnificent stained glass windows, the extent of my knowledge at that stage came from a couple of paragraphs in a Paris guidebook.

I entered the cathedral for the first time through the majestic western portal, beneath a grand relief of Christ enthroned. I gasped at the sheer enormity of the place, at the overwhelming abundance of awe-inspiring beauty contained within.

Like so many other tourists before and since, I rarely looked down after entering the cathedral. The stained glass marvels are several stories above eye level, causing visitors to bump into each other as their focus remains directed heavenward. I did not know then what is so integral to my life now: that as much glory awaited me beneath my feet as above my head. Sadly, most visitors never discover that life-changing secret.

But an unusual design on the floor had caught my eye ever so briefly when I first entered the cathedral. It niggled at the back of my mind—something about it was important—and I went back to take a second look. Embedded in the center of the floor was a large mosaic in stone, large enough for at least ten adults to stand within it. It was a type of flower, a rose with six rounded petals, and a circle in the center. Much of the ancient design had been covered with rows of chairs and was therefore difficult to see in its entirety. The rest of the pattern that surrounded this flower spanned a huge portion of the nave's floor, but this was also covered with chairs, which made it impossible to identify. What I could see of the design was beautiful and elegant but also curious. I went to stand in the central circle, at the heart of the rose, as this was the only area that was not covered with chairs.

I stood there, took a deep breath . . . and fell to my knees. A heated surge of energy flooded my body and pulled me to the ground with its force. I was dizzy for quite a while afterward, forced to sit down in the wooden chairs that covered the rest of the rose mosaic. When the dizziness wore off, I was consumed with utter fascination.

Long after my return to the States, the rose in the floor of the cathedral haunted me. That fascination became an obsession which led to a great and unexpected spiritual quest. It would become the journey of a lifetime, a journey that continues to this day.

Along my path to understanding the mystery of the rose with six petals, I discovered that the image was the central point of a huge labyrinth that extended over forty-two feet across the floor of Chartres Cathedral. The great Gothic cathedral builders in France had installed labyrinths in the floors of many of their monuments, although only a handful have survived. These are elaborate patterns built with geometric precision by master architects. They are sometimes referred to as mazes, but that is a misnomer. Mazes are places where one gets lost. Labyrinths are places where one is found.

The purpose of the labyrinths in the French cathedrals has never been definitively agreed upon by scholars or theologians. Some say that they represented a metaphorical path to the Holy Land for those in medieval times who were unable to make such a pilgrimage. Others, myself included, believe that they were created as a prayer tool, a path that could be walked while praying, toward a center where God awaits. The labyrinths all have one single path that leads in to a central place, a holy of holies reserved for prayer. I learned that Chartres Cathedral is unique in that it contains the only medieval labyrinth where the center is represented by the six-petaled rose.

In the early Middle Ages, and perhaps long before, there was a great spiritual school at Chartres. It was a center for both theology and mystery that is now the stuff of legend. The school counted saints, mystics, philosophers, politicians, and even a few infamous heretics among its

The Chartres labyrinth and the central rose with six petals

eclectic group of graduates and teachers. While much of what was taught there is lost to time and history, there are some powerful remnants of the more mystical Chartres teachings available for those who dig deeply enough.

My own search was relentless.

Thus, along my path I was fortunate enough to find teachers who invited me back in time through the ancient doors of the Chartres mystery school. They instructed me in the way of the labyrinth and showed me that the rose at the center is a portal that leads to the ultimate and most priceless treasure: spiritual transformation.

I will share some of Chartres' most potent, life-changing lessons within the pages that follow, but the essence of what I discovered is this:

The secret of the rose with six petals is its perfect correlation to the Lord's Prayer. Each petal represents a different teaching found within the prayer, and the central circle represents the essence and wellspring of LOVE, as love must feed into all aspects of our lives in order for us to achieve true fulfillment. The rose is the symbol of the perfect spiritual practice as left to us by Jesus. It is our map to the source of miracles.

The rose at the center of the labyrinth in Chartres Cathedral is the heart of an unmatched temple built to honor the power of prayer. It was central to the teachings of the medieval mystery school, and to this most powerful and sacred Christian tradition that has been nearly lost to us in modern times.

During my studies, I learned to use the Lord's Prayer as a committed practice in the same way as the students of the Chartres mystery school. Since incorporating this prayer into my daily life, I have never been the same, nor would I want to be. This practice restored my faith: in God, in myself, and in my fellow human beings.

The revelations from the Lord's Prayer that awaited me within that mystical rose changed the course of my life and that of those around me, irrevocably. They also brought the miracle that saved the life of my infant son.

SAN FRANCISCO, CALIFORNIA: MAY 2001

It was another Mother's Day, six years and six thousand miles away from Chartres. I was visiting my dear friend Stacey in the Bay Area of Northern California. It is not a coincidence that Stacey had been my companion on that fateful trip to Chartres in 1995. And like me, she had become mesmerized by the labyrinths and all that they offered in terms of spiritual progress through prayer and walking meditation. So it was on this celebratory Sunday that Stacey and I walked up the steep hill to Grace Cathedral, a San Francisco monument that contains not one but two perfect replicas of the labyrinth at Chartres and its six-petaled rose centerpiece, one on the interior and one on the exterior. We intended to walk both of the labyrinths, each for our own reasons. As an expectant mother nearing forty who had suffered terrible miscarriages, I had a lot of concerns about my pregnancy. My primary intention for these labyrinth walks was to pray for the safe delivery of the baby.

My secondary intention was to request guidance for the book I was writing at that time, a novel about the inspirational life of Mary Magdalene and her unique relationship with Jesus. I was having some faith-based challenges with that book on a number of levels. Writing about the life of Jesus was a hefty responsibility, one that sometimes overwhelmed me. Further, my research unearthed extraordinary details about Mary Magdalene's role in Jesus' life and ministry, details that are not found in traditional or academic sources. Did I have the courage to write the truth of what I had discovered? And what about the miracles that Jesus performed? How could I portray those scenes in the novel as literal, when I believed that they were meant to be viewed symbolically, as allegories? I hoped to gain clarity on these creative and spiritual challenges through the medieval prayer process. I could not have envisioned how that clarity would be delivered to me.

I was six months pregnant as I entered the labyrinth at Grace Cathedral and walked its eleven undulating circuits. Upon reaching the rose, I began to pray in earnest for my baby's health while moving through each of the petals. When I reached the center, something happened that I had never experienced before in the labyrinth: I had a vision of Mary Magdalene, who awaited me at the center. And I heard her voice, loud and clear and insistent, say to me, "No matter what anyone tells you, your baby will be fine. You will be tested, but you must know at all times that your baby will survive, and survive wholly. Do not ever believe differently, and do not ever give up. No matter what happens, you must keep your faith in this."

LOS ANGELES: AUGUST 17, 2001

Three months later, my tiny, perfect little boy was in an incubator with countless tubes and needles, none of which were helping him.

"It's nobody's fault," the social worker said to me again, still intent on convincing me that my baby was going to die and that his hospital wasn't responsible. I no longer heard him. I heard only the strong feminine voice from the labyrinth three months prior, the one that had said to me, "You will be tested, but you must know at all times that your baby will survive, and survive wholly. Do not ever believe differently, and do not ever give up. No matter what happens, you must keep your faith in this."

I had been told by the doctors that I was not to touch Shane as he was "too sensitive." But given that they also believed he was going to die any minute, I ceased to listen and took matters into my own hands. I got out of my wheelchair, pushed everyone away, and put my arms around my baby. I began to talk to him, to tell him that I would never give up on him, and I began to pray in his ear. As I did this, there was a measurable, if slight, medical response from Shane. The numbers on all the machinery he was hooked up to, previously flat and hopeless, flickered for the first time. He was fighting to stay with me, I could feel it. And I was fighting to keep him with every ounce of strength I had left. Shane was comatose and cold, small and blue and so nearly lost to us. Faith was almost all I had left, faith and love for this precious little being.

But I learned that night that those two things are all that are needed to change the world. With faith and love, all things are possible.

UCLA Medical Center is about twenty miles from the hospital where Shane was born, in Westwood Village, the college enclave in West Los Angeles. Their NICU is one of the best in the world, and they are a pioneering hospital for new, lifesaving techniques. At the insistence of my family, the doctors called UCLA as a last-ditch effort, but I was told not to get my hopes up. The life-flight helicopter wasn't available to transport us, and the UCLA team would have to come by ambulance, across town in the legendary, immovable Friday evening L.A. traffic—*if* they were even available, which was uncertain. I was assured that Shane could not possibly live long enough for the Westwood cavalry to arrive. Even if he did, through some wildly unlikely miracle, he would not survive the journey across town in the ambulance.

But I held him and prayed for the nearly two hours it took for the transport team to arrive. Shane fought along with me, holding on long enough to get out of that suburban hospital and into the hands of the angels on earth at UCLA Medical Center.

But I could not go with him.

I had just endured major surgery and experienced a few complications of my own, made worse by the unexpected, strenuous activity in the NICU. As the compassionate UCLA transport nurse took Shane from my hands to place him into their mobile incubator, the baby did something that no one anticipated. He opened his eyes.

"Impossible!" This was the exclamation from the same doctor who had nearly pronounced him dead. But Shane defied them all. He looked at me for several long seconds, and then at his distraught father, before closing his eyes again in exhaustion from the effort. In that moment, I really saw my child for the first time. He was in there, and he would come back to us. That was the first of the innumerable gifts that Shane bestowed upon us.

It was physically impossible for me to leave the hospital with Shane that night, although I wanted to desperately. I was left behind to deal with a new nightmare as the suburban doctors came in to "prepare me" for their version of the truth. They told me that because Shane was so severely oxygen-deprived, the extent of damage to his body couldn't yet be measured. His brain was affected to such a large degree that he would likely never see or hear me, much less recognize me. They said that the opening of his eyes in the NICU was simply a fluke reflex action and not to be taken as a sign of brain activity. His lungs were a nonfunctional mass that resembled scar tissue, and even if he survived, he would never be able to breathe without a respirator. His adrenal glands had hemorrhaged, and he would not be able to produce the hormones necessary to live and grow. It was likely that his other organs were in similar states of irreparable destruction.

One doctor actually said to me, "It isn't necessarily a good thing that your baby lived through the night."

I wish I could report that my faith was so strong that I never believed any of this, but I would be lying. I hadn't seen the miracles that would give me that kind of utterly unshakable faith yet. I was still being tested.

That was the darkest night of my life. My poor, suffering baby was across the city and I couldn't be with him. I was alone in this wretched place with worst-case scenario news from the doctors, while my family was with the baby in a neonatal intensive care unit across town. I had never known such misery, or fear.

The next day, I checked out of that hospital and joined my family at my baby's bedside, where I stayed for the next twelve days.

We never left the baby, except for the hour a day when the patient NICU nurses changed shifts. Perhaps it was a coincidence that three of Shane's primary care nurses were named Mary, Magdalena, and Mary Ann. But each of these women was blessed with the compassion and grace of their namesakes, and it was with their support that we kept our vigil.

We lived in armchairs at the side of Shane's bed, talking to him, singing to him, and most of all, praying. We prayed in the NICU, we prayed in the hospital chapel, we prayed in the garden, and we invited our friends and family all over the world to pray with us via telephone and Internet. There were thousands of people praying for our baby. We never gave up.

The Lord's Prayer was my anchor through this difficult time, and I envisioned the rose as I meditated. I struggled to have faith and to surrender to the will of God, which are the tasks of the first and second petals in the prayer practice, every single day. In order to get through the ordeal, I had to believe that all of this was happening for a reason, so I clung tightly to that faith. And I used the rest of the Lord's Prayer practice as necessary. Sometimes I had to get through major financial worries: we couldn't afford not to work during this time, and yet leaving the baby was not an option. Whatever the outcome, it was certain that we were going to eventually go home to a financial crisis. At other times I had to deal with my anger over the circumstances and even find forgiveness for the doctors who had almost let my baby die. These weighty burdens were made far more bearable through the prayer. And all the while I clung to the vision from the labyrinth and the message that I must not give up.

On the twelfth night in the NICU, I got up to take a walk. I was sore from sleeping in the chair, and in pain from the huge abdominal incision that had not been given the proper time and opportunity to heal. I refused to take pain medication because I did not want to numb my brain or spirit through this experience. Shane might need me at any moment, and he would need me to be fully present. I walked the halls for a few minutes before realizing that it didn't help, so I returned to the NICU and my post at my baby's bedside.

The NICU at that time was a large, open room, and Shane's bed was on the left at the far corner. As I looked toward his area, I could see it was surrounded by a soft light. At first I thought that there was a doctor or nurse working on him, as I could also see someone leaning over the bed. But as I walked a few steps closer, I stopped short at what I saw ahead of me.

There was a beautiful man with long hair leaning over my baby's bed.

Now, Shane's father, Peter, is a beautiful man with long hair, so I thought for a moment that this was he. But I quickly saw that Peter was asleep in the chair on the other side of Shane's bed.

I don't know how long I stood there; it is a moment lost in time, and yet completely etched into my brain, heart, and spirit for eternity. I watched the man lean over and kiss my baby on the top of his head. And then . . . he was simply gone.

The next day, Shane opened his eyes.

I will never be able to completely account for what happened in the days after that incident. They are a blur of joy and shock, astonishment and gratitude. All I can say is that on September 2, 2001, we took our baby boy home as if he had been born brand-new and entirely healthy the day before. It seemed that he had regenerated his organs, and his lungs were perfect.

UCLA enrolled Shane into a two-year study with a complex name that involved the plasticity of the newborn brain, a study that perhaps seeks to quantify that which is unquantifiable. Shane had MRIs and ultrasounds and many other tests throughout the first years of his life. He was seen and analyzed by some of the great minds in neonatal medicine. But the medical professionals involved agreed on one thing: although the brilliance of modern medicine had kept Shane alive and must not be discounted, his regenerated organs were almost entirely unexplainable. There was a factor in this case that transcended science.

Pure and simple, Shane was a living miracle.

While we were all prepared to celebrate, there was one outstanding health issue that required follow-up. We remained cautiously optimistic, because although Shane had inexplicably repaired his lungs and his brain, there appeared to be a lingering problem with his adrenal glands. One was completely destroyed and beyond redemption. The second was functional but also damaged. Our first visit to a pediatric endocrinologist immediately dampened the celebration of Shane's survival. The doctor's prognosis was dire and his manner harsh as he told us that he didn't think Shane would live past the age of two. His adrenals were too far gone, and as such, he could not produce the hormones needed to sustain life. The worst-case scenario had returned.

It was a serious blow that threatened to set us all back and into that place of despair. But after all that we had been through, I refused to believe yet another death sentence dealt to my baby boy. I held fast to my faith and continued to pray, all the while searching out the best doctors in pediatric medicine. I believe firmly that science and faith can and should coexist beautifully, and I lived by that philosophy throughout Shane's early childhood. My oldest brother, Kelly, is a gifted obstetrician who has taught me a great deal through the example of his own brilliant, scientific mind. He helped me to find the best doctors to ensure that Shane had the benefit of state-of-the-art science at the same time that our family continued our prayer-based spiritual approach.

There is an old story about a family clinging to a rowboat during a flood: they prayed together fervently, but they also rowed as hard as they could. It is an example of faith in action and illustrative of the wise old adage, "The Lord helps those who help themselves."

Over the next two years, sonograms of Shane's adrenal glands proved that the miracles had not ceased. The right adrenal gland was not only functioning perfectly, but the previously destroyed gland on the left had been completely regenerated from nothing. Apparently, both Shane and God were just taking their time to ensure that we were all on our way to understanding the lesson here thoroughly:

Miracles happen, and they are real, physical, and unlimited.

When I was praying during those dark days of our journey with Shane, I would meditate often on the third petal of the rose at the center of the labyrinth, the petal that represents the path of service and the line in the Lord's Prayer: *As in heaven, so upon earth.* I took a vow that when we got through this challenge, I would one day help others by sharing our miracle with the world. I later posted Shane's story on the Internet, and over the years I have received emails from families who told me that it gave them hope in their darkest moments—and encouraged them to pray for their own miracles. There is even one special little boy in Chicago whose family credits Shane's story as instrumental to his own miraculous survival of a similar ailment.

As I write this book, Shane has just celebrated his seventh birthday. He is the most beautiful, brilliant, happy little boy in the world. He has never had a complication or been ill beyond the normal colds that occur in all children, and even those have been few and far between.

And Shane recites the Lord's Prayer perfectly, every day of his blessed, miraculous life.

THE SOURCE OF MIRACLES

Remember back in San Francisco, on Mother's Day of 2001, when I went to Grace Cathedral to walk the labyrinth? When I was having faith-based issues surrounding my novel about Jesus' life with Mary Magdalene? At the time of Shane's birth, I was writing about the miracles accredited to Jesus in the New Testament as a key element in that book. In those naïve times, I was trying to write about those miracles as metaphors. Of course, we weren't really expected to believe that Jesus turned barrels of water into the finest wine, and we certainly weren't expected to accept that he was able to feed five thousand people with two fish and a few loaves of bread! The raising of Lazarus was also symbolic: it represented *spiritual* rebirth, not a literal raising from the dead. No twenty-first-century intellect was really going to believe that such miracles were *real*, right? They were all meant to be *allegorical*, right?

And then there was Shane.

Shane's healing—his complete regeneration of the organs in his body—was not a metaphor. It was not an allegory. It was a genuine, physical miracle. And I believe that one of Shane's many gifts was in showing me that *the power of prayer is the source of miracles*. He helped me to grasp that Jesus, as the greatest master of prayer in human history, certainly knew the source for such things. And in his great compassion and love for us, Jesus gifted us with the most foolproof formula for accessing that source.

That formula, that access, is through the Lord's Prayer.

The source is unlimited. The miracles never cease.

III

How to Use This Book

*C*aution: *Committed use* of this process can bring about happiness, abundance, and fulfillment beyond your wildest expectations.

The subtitle of this book claims that *the prayer will transform your life*. It's a hefty claim, but I believe it is also an honest one. It is, in fact, the intention of the Lord's Prayer and the practice that surrounds it.

But the key to your success with this practice is *commitment*.

I am about to introduce you to the most powerful tool for changing your life—and changing the world—that you will likely ever encounter. However, there are a few disclosures and guidelines that you need to be aware of here at the outset.

There is a hard fact that we have to deal with up front, so here it is: *there is no such thing as instant gratification in the world of the spirit*. Real change requires real effort and dedication. This is not "fast-food" spirituality like so many of the techniques that have become popular recently. Those instant manifestation programs may make you feel good by satisfying your initial hunger, but they will ultimately leave you nutritionally deprived and bloated a few hours later, rather like a double cheeseburger and a hot apple turnover washed down with a thirty-two-ounce bucket of soda.

Would you like fries with your instant manifestation?

The market is flooded these days with books and DVDs on the laws of attraction and how to manifest unlimited abundance. These programs promise instant gratification. If you can imagine that Ferrari in the driveway and really feel like you can have it, then you can. Ask, believe, receive! It's that simple!

Is it? Really?

Remember the old cliché that if it sounds too good to be true, it probably is? Well, I'm willing to bet that quite a few of you reading this now have also read those manifestation books. I'm also willing to bet that there is no Ferrari in your driveway. Even if you asked and believed, you likely didn't receive. And here is the simple reason: *those other techniques do not require any kind of accountability and therefore they do not work.* Period. They tell you that you can have whatever you want with no responsibility and no consequences. But one great truth of the law of abundance is this: *you cannot manifest something that is not in the best interest of the world around you.* You do not live in a vacuum, you live on a planet with almost seven billion other people. In order to manifest everything that you desire, you must learn how to live in harmony with the bigger picture and find your own place in God's plan as a member of the human family. Of course, becoming aligned with your own spiritual nature and destiny will likely change the specifics of what you truly desire, making it that much easier to attain.

What we are reaching for here is something deeper, something that endures in your life for years after you turn the last page. That is the essence of transformation. In the following chapters, you will be asked to dig down into the deepest recesses of your heart and soul. You will be asked to examine your beliefs about yourself, about God, and about your fellow human beings. Because it is in understanding the synergy of those relationships—the truth that we are all connected and must work together—that you will find dramatic results. It is not enough to know *what* you want, you must also know *why* you want it, and what you will do once you have it! All those elements impact the world around you and therefore must be considered.

The greater the commitment you are willing to make to this process, the faster and more dramatic your transformation will be. Saying the Lord's Prayer tonight is not going to make your life look entirely different when you wake up tomorrow. But using the prayer as a spiritual practice on a consistent basis in the way presented here will be more effective than any magic words, visualization technique, or "secret" that you have ever read about before.

Jesus said, *"Ask and it is given, knock and it is opened to you."* But those words have been misinterpreted and mangled by those who would peddle the concept of instant manifestation from the movie screen, television, and bookshelves. While I assume that the many modern teachers of these laws of attraction and abundance are well-intentioned, the fact remains that what they are preaching simply doesn't work. Jesus was not giving us a genie in a lamp to jump out and grant our wildest desires in unlimited wishes—and for good reason.

There are many fascinating fables from ancient and modern literature about humans who are given the opportunity to make free and unfettered wishes. In every single tale, the wisher comes to some ill. Calamity and misfortune follow them as a result of their wishes. Often, the moral deals with greed, but the larger if more subtle theme is isolation. When we wish for something without considering the whole of the world around us, we are not honoring our place as a member of a larger human family. God's family.

Unfortunately, those who quote the *Ask and it is given* verse for the purposes of instant manifestation rarely discuss it in the context that Jesus presented it. The passages that precede it contain extensive instructions for living a good and responsible life so that we may then "ask"—and subsequently "receive"—as a reward for living in harmony with God's plan.

There is extraordinarily good news here, even if it takes a little more work to find it than we may have originally been led to believe. Jesus *was* giving us the key to unlocking the mysteries of the universe through perfecting our souls and answering to God. He *did* teach us that we can manifest everything we need and want in our lives, if we follow the rules set out for us. And he also gave us the tools to use for that purpose.

The skeleton key that unlocks every door is the Lord's Prayer.

MAKE THE COMMITMENT

Do you want to transform your life so that you wake up every day excited about what awaits you—free from worry and full of joy? Do you want to improve the world around you and help others to find the same kind of happiness and freedom? You absolutely can, but you need to commit. Here and now, you need to decide that you are going to dedicate your mind and spirit to this prayer practice. The word *decide* comes from the Latin verb *decidere*, which means "to cut off." When you decide that you are going to do something, you cut off every other possibility. I want this prayer process to work for you, and it will if you *decide* to make a commitment to it. But as you will see in the chapter about petal six, complacency is the devil. Anything that stops you from fulfilling your life's highest purpose and distracts from your faith can be counted as *evil*. You cannot allow yourself to get complacent and just coast through life. And once you see the power of this prayer in action, you won't likely ever want to do that.

As a wise teacher once said, "Miracles happen to those who believe in them." Within this spiritual practice, you will be reminded to celebrate each success and acknowledge every synchronicity that comes your way. The more you express recognition of the divine orchestration happening in your life, the faster the positive changes will occur. It's like magic. Only better.

Remember that when Jesus walked the earth, he often said he was speaking to those with ears to hear and eyes to see. It sometimes takes a little effort to read all the rich layers that exist in his lines, but the reward for this work will be an abundance beyond your current imaginings. The prayer is so perfect that it will meet the seeker in his or her own place of seeking. For example, the pilgrim who is new on the path will find it completely accessible and easy to comprehend, yet the advanced spiritual student will achieve equally powerful results in its use.

While this prayer was first taught by Jesus Christ, you do not have to be a Christian to use it. One of the more revolutionary aspects of Jesus' life was that he did not discriminate in his teachings; he preached that the kingdom of God was for everyone. He taught all denominations and ethnicities, men and women, the healthy and the sick, and those who were seen as "unclean" by his society. Jesus found everyone worthy as he recognized us all as his family under God. Thus there is a pure, universal nature to this prayer and the practice that accompanies it. It is essentially nondenominational, and I have shared this practice with friends from Jewish, Muslim, Buddhist, and even pagan backgrounds. You do not have to be a practicing Christian to use this process. You simply have to believe in a higher power and believe that your life has a purpose within that higher power.

Whatever your perspective is on Jesus—God, man, prophet, teacher—there is no denying his singular importance in shaping the world. No other figure in history has had such impact or inspired as much literature. It is in exploring the many, varied sources within that literature that we can begin to grasp the essence of the priceless gift that Jesus left for us. In this book I quote extensively from the Gospels of Matthew and Luke but also from a number of other early Christian writings that shaped my own spiritual journey while walking the labyrinth of medieval mysteries.

In Matthew 23, verses 8–12, Jesus cautions his apostles, *"And you are not to be called teachers because you have only one Teacher. . . . You are not to be called leader for One is your leader. . . . Whoever exalts himself will be humbled and whoever humbles himself will be exalted."* I took that verse to heart as I wrote this book. I am not a guru or a master or an earnest New Age leader. I am a seeker after truth and peace, and a laborer for God. I strive to be your sister on the path and to share my experiences with you, because I learned this process most profoundly through living it. This prayer and the practice surrounding it are ancient, but they transformed my life in a most modern way. I want to give you access to that same gift, in a much shorter period of time. The world is at critical mass, and we need to clean things up fast, starting with extraordinary transformation in our individual lives and then working toward global change. We don't have time for everyone to learn at my slow pace!

In Jesus' time, his words inspired people who lived amid great chaos and disillusionment. In the twenty-first century, we find ourselves in trying circumstances of perhaps a similar nature: war, famine, genocide, crime, economic collapse, and corruption fill the headlines of our newspapers. Jesus provided a tool of grace for his own embattled world and he provided one for us in our time. The Lord's Prayer is timeless; it has as much application now, if not more, than it had when it was first spoken in Galilee and Jerusalem.

The Lord's Prayer is our instruction manual for creating heaven on earth, and while the prayer is only a few lines long, the layers of meaning within it could fill volumes. The greatest of the medieval minds knew how to find that meaning, and they have left that gift to us as their legacy, in the stone of their cathedrals and in the memory of their teachings.

FOLLOW THE ORDER—— AND WORK WITH INTENTION

The Lord's Prayer contains six primary teachings, with a seventh that must be present throughout the practice, and that is *love*. The six main teachings correspond with the six petals of the rose at the center of the Chartres labyrinth, with the seventh in the center, radiating through all the others. In the beginning, it is most important that you take these lessons in order, as each segues into the next. For example, you should not jump right into the fourth petal, which represents abundance, until you have worked through the first three: faith, surrender, and service.

Only after you have performed the practices in the first three lessons will the fourth be effective. You cannot have effortless abundance unless you earn it, and you earn it through faith, surrender, and service.

There is a reason that abundance is the fourth teaching, and not the first. Putting abundance first would be similar to sending a teenager into a master's or doctoral program before he completed basic college courses. The student is simply not ready and doesn't have the foundation necessary to master the more complex teachings to come. Manifestation programs that tell you to skip directly to asking for whatever you want are not only misleading, they actually set back your spiritual growth and make it much harder for you to find abundance on any level. This danger is discussed in greater length in the chapter on abundance, the fourth petal.

Nothing comes for free, either in matter or in spirit! But when you work for something and truly earn it, the feeling of fulfillment is that much greater.

So while the abundance technique that you will focus on as you reach the fourth petal will likely be the most powerful manifestation tool you will ever use, it will only be so if you have completed the three lessons that precede it. Once you have mastered the techniques and understand the lessons in all six petals, you will be able to select whichever lesson you feel the need to work on from day to day. It will become second nature to you. But as a beginner, you must work through them *in order* to attain the greatest result. The rose is the sum of its parts. If you were to pull the petals from a rose one at a time, you would lose the natural beauty of the flower. But if you view the petals together as they were created, you will be rewarded with something truly lovely.

An important word about what Jesus himself warned of: "vain repetitions." Reciting any prayer by rote, with no feeling or understanding, just to get credit for saying it, is a vain repetition. It is utterly useless, a waste of time, and quite possibly offensive to divine intelligence. When we mumble prayers we sound bored and lifeless; there is no soul in the words, and that is most definitely missing the point.

So when you decide to undertake this practice, don't just show up. Show up with passion. Show up with intention. Show up and mean it.

Take a vow from this day forward that if you are going to pray, you will pray with intelligence and heart and spirit, utilizing the glorious faculties which were generously provided to you upon your birth into this beautiful world. God gave us everything we need within ourselves to manifest a perfect, abundant, happy, love-filled life, to feel great and have fun while doing it. He is our divine parent who desires only to see his children prosper. The Lord's Prayer is his handbook for fulfillment, and the rose with six petals is the map that guides us through it.

THE PROCESS

This book is organized into seven chapters, each representing a primary teaching related to lines from the prayer. Within each of these chapters are a series of questions, challenging inquiries designed to make you dig deep into your heart as you examine your life. Chapters also include meditations, affirmations, and other recommended activities that will help you align to the lessons within the prayer. Some will seem simple, while you may feel more resistance to others or find that some will require more time and focus. Everyone will have a different experience with these practices depending on the current circumstances in their lives. The prayer will always meet you where you are living in that moment. The amount of time and depth that you spend in contemplation of these questions will correlate directly with the transformational power of the prayer in your life. I recommend that you write the answers and keep them in a journal, either by hand or electronically. Looking back on the notes you have made, and thereby witnessing your own spiritual progress, reinforces the teachings and can be very rewarding.

There are a number of ways that you can work with the imagery of the six-petaled rose. You can use the illustrations in this book as visual references. You can go to my website and print out a free copy of the rose to put up on your wall or keep on your desk. Personally, I invested in a prayer mat that contains the six petals so that I can stand in them as I pray, moving into each petal with the corresponding lines of the prayer just as the medieval mystery school students once did. I am also creating a six-petaled rose out of paving stones in my garden, which is fun and inexpensive. Another inexpensive option is to buy children's sidewalk chalk and draw your own six-petaled rose, either on an outside surface or on a large floor mat. Be creative! Remember that the word *create* comes from the same origin as *Creator*, so we are closer to God when we are using our creativity.

Each chapter also contains affirmations that can help you work through particularly challenging elements. For example, in the chapter on petal five, the path of forgiveness, we are reminded that *people are doing the best they can with what they have.* I use that mantra each time somebody disappoints me, whether it's a good friend or a retail clerk who gives me particularly poor service. You'll be surprised how much that affirmation can help you to move past issues that would normally irritate you. I recommend that you write out the affirmations you need and tape them in key areas as reminders: your computer, your bathroom mirror, anywhere that you spend significant time. These aids are particularly helpful when you are working through this process in tandem with friends, family, or partners, as they will understand and support your new philosophy!

On that note, I encourage you to enlist others to join you on this path so that you may begin the process together. The more support that surrounds you, the faster you will see the results in your life. Just as I was writing this, I said something rather derogatory about an acquaintance while complaining to a friend. Granted, the person in question has caused our family huge amounts of stress and disruption, but that is perhaps the challenge I am meant to experience; can I love others consistently, even when they are behaving in a most unlovable manner? It's hard! But my friend immediately set me straight by reminding me, "That comment wasn't exactly loving or forgiving, now, was it?" He was right, of course. Anger breeds anger and forgiveness breeds forgiveness. And having a companion on the same path helped me to shift my focus out of anger and into forgiveness.

People are doing the best they can with what they have, and that includes this acquaintance who has caused me such annoyance. Now, had I made the original complaint to someone else, who wasn't a participant in this practice with me, it is likely the response would have been something like, "Oh, yeah. She certainly is a you-know-what," and we would spend a good few minutes continuing to bash this person who was behaving in a particularly unlovable manner. The anger would be fed and the negativity would grow. That is the usual course of events.

Stay within the teachings of the Lord's Prayer, even when challenged. Especially when challenged.

You will be challenged often! I know I am, almost daily. None of us are saints, and most of us probably don't have any aspirations to become one, what with all the messy inconveniences of martyrdom. But we can become better humans and lead richer lives simply by shifting our attitudes. We can't control the behavior of others, but we can control our actions and reactions around that behavior. And your actions, when they are loving, forgiving, and in harmony with creating a better world, *will change your life in the most magnificent ways*. If we can all learn to value the lessons in this prayer, we just might save the world.

DAILY USE OF THE LORD'S PRAYER

Your practice from this day forward will include reciting the Lord's Prayer every day at least once, slowly and deliberately, while really thinking about what each phrase means and feeling every one of the words as you say them. The chapters that follow break the prayer down in a way that analyzes and explains just how rich and rewarding the legacy of this prayer is. I hope that it will bring you the unlimited joy and abundance that it has brought me, and that above all it provides you with a true understanding of how great a gift Jesus was leaving to all of us in this unequaled prayer.

As you work through the chapters of this book, you will find that certain issues stand out for you at this time in your life. Focus on those elements that move you. There is only one hard-and-fast rule in carrying out this process: make the commitment and carve out time for yourself every day to pray. This does not have to be a prolonged process. Some days you may want to spend a lot of time on it; other days you simply can't. That's fine, as long as you do *something* every single day. If I told you that you can have absolutely everything you ever desired in your life by just reserving five to ten minutes a day for a simple practice, wouldn't you do it?

When I am out of sorts, depressed, angry, or feeling helpless in any way, I can always find the cause in one thing: I have not been keeping up with my prayer practice. Every single time that I fall into one of these dark moods, it is because I have lapsed. I am busy and harried and overcommitted just like everyone else. Sometimes between trying to get kids off to school, the dog walked, dinner in the oven, a reasonable amount of writing accomplished, and hundreds of emails read, I lose time for myself—and God. I'm guessing you can relate.

You cannot neglect the practice and still find the inner peace and life-changing transformation that you seek. You must make time for yourself. Five to ten minutes a day is all it takes. Sometimes I do it at night when everyone else is asleep and the house is quiet; other times I find it a great way to start the day and do it first thing in the morning. Depending on the time of day and the weather, sometimes I pray inside, sometimes outside. You can create a designated space for your practice so it feels more ceremonial to you; set up an altar in your home, or create a six-petaleded rose space in your garden. You can be as simple or as elaborate as you choose. The beauty of this process is that it requires nothing but your commitment! Regardless of how or where you decide to do it, it must be done. You owe it to yourself, you owe it to the people you love, and you owe it to God.

Here are the basic steps to using this prayer regularly:

- Each day you will begin in exactly the same way. Take a few deep breaths. Relax. Allow the strains of the day to melt away with each breath, breathing in relaxation, and pushing out any residual stress with forceful exhalations. Affirm in your mind that you are entering into a place of love, a place where God hears and feels everything you have to say.

- Speak the prayer aloud, slowly and with thought to every line, all the way through without stopping. Then speak it again, this time envisioning the six-petaled rose and pausing at every one of the six teachings (you will discover each in order and detail within the following chapters). If there is something you need to work on within that specific petal, pray for it there. Talk to God and tell him what you need or what is bothering you. If you are feeling particularly secure in one teaching, move on to the next.

- Allow the events of each individual day to inform your prayer process. Some days you will really need to work on surrender, on turning all your worries over to God. Other days you may need to release anger or envy or find forgiveness.

- Use the affirmations in this book to help you focus on those issues that are most important to you, and feel free to supplement with other prayers (see the affirmations and prayer index at the back of this book).

- Always express your love and gratitude to God at the end of each session. I personally end each prayer with *Thy will, not mine, be done*.

These are suggestions based on how I work through the prayer on a daily basis. The more you incorporate this prayer practice into your life, the more it will evolve into something natural and easy for you. It can be a tremendous respite. I find prolonged moments in prayer to be more restful than a vacation and better than a day at the spa!

Make time for God and make time for yourself. Through this process you will find your way to the unlimited source of miracles. Welcome. We've been waiting for you.

To pray is not to prevent winter, but to allow summer.

The Gospel of Philip

IV

What Is Prayer?

*S*omething *magical happens* when we pray that I certainly cannot explain. I am happy enough to stand in awe of the divine and to celebrate its presence on earth every single day. But I do know that prayer creates miracles. I know that prayer transforms lives and changes the world. And I know, not because of blind faith, but because I have witnessed it at work, over and over again.

Theologians around the world and through time have filled pages on the nature of prayer. I will give you my own very simple definition here:

> *P*rayer *is our means of celebrating God while reinforcing our connection to the divine and our destinies to create a world on earth as it is in heaven.*

When we pray, we reinforce our faith. We put our energy toward God and goodness and helping others. That can only bring about positive results. When we pray for someone other than ourselves, we increase that power exponentially. While Shane was in intensive care, there were groups all over the world, from all denominations, praying for him. I don't just believe that those prayers impacted his healing—I am certain of it. I have seen the miracles wrought by "prayer circles" on many occasions. For a number of years I hosted a spiritual discussion forum online with about six hundred members. An impromptu "prayer group" arose out of that community. When anyone had a specific worry or ailment—some life-threatening, others less dire, but all important to the individual requesting aid—we would agree to pray for that person. Time and again in the microcosm of my little online world, we saw the powerful and positive impact of these group prayers. I could write books about all the miracles I have witnessed and never run out of material.

The power at work here, the force behind all prayer, is love: love for each other and love for God, which is what Jesus repeatedly emphasized as the two greatest of all commandments.

THY WILL, NOT MINE, BE DONE

Note that my definition does not say that prayer is a place where we ask God to give us things. I'm not saying that you can't or shouldn't ask God for what you need. I'm saying that this shouldn't be the only time that you pray! Many people pray *only* when they want something. Prayer is a way for us to get closer to God, to celebrate God's presence in our lives. We should pray every day for the sheer joy of it. When it is a regular practice, your prayer requests will be that much more powerful when you do make them.

We are not closer to God when we are blindly asking for something.

We are closer to God when our prayer is made in the spirit of *thy will, not mine, be done.* This is why Jesus tells us exactly how to pray in Matthew and Luke. He wants us to understand how it must be done to be effective. The true secret to creating miracles through a successful prayer practice is constant alignment to your highest source, your reason for being here on earth, your service to God's higher good for the planet and its people.

God is many things, but one of these is Divine Intelligence, which is infinite and therefore unfathomable to the human mind. We can contemplate infinity, but we cannot know it. An aspect of faith is realizing that God is much more than we can possibly imagine, and accepting that greatness without challenging it. Every time I think of the synchronicities that occur on a daily basis to get us where we need to be, of the divine orchestration at play in our lives that ensures we meet the right people at the right time, I am in awe.

I was just listening to an atheist comedian on television ridiculing the power of prayer. He asked, "How is it possible that one being can listen to billions of people mumbling prayers and actually differentiate between all of them? Or care about what they are asking, much less act on it?"

I have to admit that our disbelieving comic has a point for those who are still in a place of questioning. Because there *is* a legitimate question here to be explored, even for the faithful.

Here is how I have come to answer this question. God listens, hears, and responds to all prayers—*as long as you are praying in the proper spirit.* To put it most simply: you must speak the right language. When you are praying in a manner that is in harmony with the divine mind, you are heard and your prayers are fulfilled. The miracles flow naturally to you from the unlimited source, which is God.

Anything that is inharmonious to God—ego-driven, greedy, or otherwise "sinfully" motivated—goes unheard and unfulfilled. This type of false prayer falls into the category that Jesus described as "babbling."

So how do you assure that you are praying in the proper spirit? By following the instructions laid out for you by Jesus as discussed in the following pages. Pray for the healing of others often and freely, as you will be instructed, and when you pray for yourself, always finish the prayer with some version of "in a manner that is in harmony with your divine will" or the phrase I use, "Thy will, not mine, be done." These methods will be discussed in the chapters on petal two, surrender, and petal four, abundance. If you pray in the spirit of surrender, in the clear understanding that you are here to create heaven on earth, you will be heard by the divine mind.

LORD, TEACH US TO PRAY

Jesus had a lot to say about the nature of prayer, particularly while delivering the Sermon on the Mount to his followers in Galilee, which is where the Lord's Prayer was first introduced. The sermon itself represents the summation of all Jesus' teachings. Within it, he taught the secrets of life in a pure and simple form. But it is the Lord's Prayer that stands out as the single most important lesson of Jesus' ministry.

Jesus gives us very specific instructions about prayer in the Gospel of Matthew, chapter 6, verses 5–15:

"And when you pray, do not be like the hypocrites, for they love to pray . . . on the street corners to be seen by men. . . . But when you pray, go into your room, close the door and pray to your Father. . . . Then your Father, who sees what is done in secret, will reward you. And when you pray, do not keep on babbling. . . . for your Father knows what you need before you ask him. This, then, is how you should pray:

> *'Our father in heaven,*
> *may your name be hallowed,*
> *may your kingdom come,*
> *may your will be done,*
> *as in heaven, so upon earth.*
> *Give us today our sufficient bread,*
> *and forgive us our debts,*
> *as we also have forgiven our debtors.*
> *And do not bring us into temptation,*
> *but deliver us from evil.' "*

It is important to note that different translations substitute the word *trespasses* and sometimes *sin* in place of *debt*. Equally interesting is that Jesus ends the prayer with this powerful spiritual reminder about forgiveness that is usually left off and forgotten in the context of teaching the Lord's Prayer.

"For if you forgive men when they sin against you, your heavenly Father will also forgive you. But if you do not forgive men their sins, your Father will not forgive your sins."

Later, in the Gospel of Luke, Jesus is asked by one of his disciples, "*Lord, teach us to pray*." He responds again very specifically, with the

Lord's Prayer. So we see in scripture that *when Jesus teaches us to pray, it is always with these words*.

The prayer is perfect. It is our greatest spiritual gift, from the great spiritual giver.

There is no mystery here, no secret. Jesus literally shouted from a mountaintop the only magic words we will ever need to live a life of perfect joy and unlimited abundance!

Two thousand years later, isn't it finally time that we listened?

"Before you were formed in the womb, I knew you."

Jeremiah 1:5

V

The First Petal—Faith

Faith

he first petal of the rose corresponds to these words of the prayer:

> *Our father in heaven,*
> *may your name be hallowed,*

Faith is the foundation for transformational spiritual practice, and it is the starting point for all prayer. It is in this first lesson where you must begin to define the nature of your faith and your relationship with God. The stronger the foundation, the more enduring the structure will be that is built upon it. Within the lessons of the first petal, you will be asked to contemplate your image of who and what God is in your life and to answer a series of questions designed to inspire deep introspection about your faith. Establishing your strongest connection to your Creator is vital before moving forward into the critical question that awaits on the path of the first petal: Why are you here? What is the meaning of your life? What is your specific role and purpose in God's plan?

The foundational lesson of the first petal is to understand and accept that you are part of the Creator's master plan. As such, you have a specific role to play; you made a "promise" to God before you were born. While working through the teachings of the first petal, you will be asked the deepest and most challenging questions of the entire practice: What was the promise you made to God before your birth? What role did you joyously accept? Are you on the path of fulfilling your promise?

You will be asked further to contemplate the more human aspects of your faith: faith in yourself and faith in your fellow humans, as both must exist as you continue along the path toward fulfillment and unlimited happiness.

Didn't I warn you that we were going to dig deep here?

OUR FATHER

Our father. It doesn't sound revolutionary, does it? But it is. And it certainly would have been during the time in which Jesus lived. Each of those two words, as simple as they may seem, was deliberately selected to convey a separate and powerful concept. But look first at the words in combination. They are, in their simplicity, a perfect expression of exactly who and what God is: *our father*.

He is our benevolent parent, the perfect, divine father who loves us unconditionally and without compromise. Jesus was telling us with these two simple words that God is not a jealous tyrant to be feared but a loving and protective essence. This concept, as simple as it sounds, was revolutionary, even dangerous, in Jesus' own time. It was a time when the Old Testament God of fear and retribution, a God who professed that he was jealous, reigned supreme.

Before going any further, let's address an issue that is becoming very common in twenty-first-century spirituality so that no one gets so hung up that they can't progress through the rest of this life-changing process. A recent and surprising study conducted by the Harris Poll indicated that *over half of Americans questioned did not believe that God was necessarily male*. Only 34 percent asserted that God was definitively masculine. The idea that God is neither male nor singular but is instead perhaps both male and female is gaining more believers in our time. In other words, if there is an *our father*, is there also an *our mother*? And if there is, shouldn't she be included in the prayer? Some modern theologians claim that the early Aramaic and Syriac versions of the prayer may have actually referred to God as our divine creator, who is both mother and father. As always in areas of biblical scholarship, there is much heated debate about this.

But in the way that as human children we petition our parents differently, the same is true of prayer. Think about it: did you go to your mother for help in the same way that you approached your father? Or did you speak to different parents for individual requests, and in varying ways? Did you hit up Dad when you wanted cash but run to Mom when you needed a hug? This distinction relates to the archetypal nature of father and mother: father as provider, mother as nurturer.

Thus for the purposes of this book and in keeping with the original medieval teachings of the rose, I am staying with *our father* and will continue to relate to God in this context as male. I do this because I absolutely believe that Jesus was addressing this issue within the prayer itself.

If you are one of those millions of believers who envision God as both male and female, I invite you to consider the Lord's Prayer specifically as a petition to your father, the male side of the loving parental essence. In this case, the provider. You are not excluding your mother; you are simply addressing your father. I have written books celebrating the nature of God as both male and female and the return of the divine feminine element as critical to our spiritual growth, and even to the greater goal of peace in the twenty-first century. I therefore understand that there may be resistance from many of you who feel that this prayer on the surface feels patriarchal or exclusionary. I assure you that it is not.

And yet, I do not think that it matters to God how you perceive this piece of the prayer. As previously stated, this is not a jealous, petty, and spiteful divine being. This is the pure essence of love and caring. The first petal is the place to contemplate all aspects of your faith, so stop here for a moment and think about this issue of God's essence.

Exercise: **What Is Your Relationship with God?**
Answer the following questions as thoroughly and honestly as possible.

- What does God look like or feel like in your understanding?
- Does the issue of God and gender matter to you? Do you feel that God is male, female, or both? Or neither?
- Can you respect and accept someone else's image of God, even if it is different from your own?
- Can you approach God as your father and petition him in that way

for the purposes of this prayer practice? If not, what kind of adjustments do you need to make to continue?

In understanding that God is our father, we are given another key piece of wisdom: what is in the parent is in the child. Just as we carry the traits of our parents here on earth, so do we carry the traits of our parent in heaven. We have divinity in us. We are not God, but we are the offspring of our divine creator, and therefore we carry the nature of those heavenly origins. There is an old Irish expression, "What's in the cat is in the kitten." Jesus says this, too, in a number of different passages. He asks us, "Do people pick grapes from thorn bushes or figs from thistles?" And then he reminds us, "Every good tree bears good fruit." We are reminded that the child is always an expression of the parent's essence.

Thus, the omnipotent, omniscient, omnipresent power of the universe is your father and he wants what is best for you and to help you find happiness. He is not an unreachable and fearsome old man in the sky, and he is not a dictator. He is your parent, and he loves and cares about you and wants you to experience that love on a daily basis. Your father does not require that you use a middleman to reach him. He wants you to have a personal relationship with him. He wants you to feel his love, and he wants to feel yours in return. This connection is achieved most effectively through prayer.

The very first word of the Lord's Prayer sets the tone and delivers the key message that Jesus wanted us to grasp immediately: *our*. Jesus did not say *my* father, and he did not say *your* father. He said *our* father. It is both plural and inclusive. This word choice is precise and made with intention, as it is the underlying premise of a great understanding: that we are all brothers and sisters, with one common parent. When we look at ourselves collectively, as the children of our father, there is no separation. We are all related within the human family, and we are being called to remember that and to treat all mankind as our brothers and sisters. Just as our earthly parents want their children to live in harmony, our heavenly parent wants us to do the same.

Furthermore, by using the word *our*, Jesus is telling us that we are not separate from him either. Jesus is not above us and untouchable. Rather he is beside us, like a sibling, side by side with us in reverence to the divine will, intelligence, and love which is our father. Jesus was sent to be our master guide in the process. He is our older, wiser, protective brother.

From the opening word, Jesus emphasized that the Lord's Prayer is universally inclusive. We are all one tribe, one global human family under God.

Exercise: **Embracing Your Divine Parent and Earthly Siblings**
Answer the following questions as thoroughly and honestly as possible.

- How does looking at God as your benevolent parent change your perspective or otherwise impact your faith? Does it differ from the faith you were raised in? How?
- How does the understanding of God as our father change your relationship to other human beings?
- How do you feel about accepting Jesus as your brother and also as a loving and entirely accessible force in your life? Does it differ from the faith you were raised in? How?
- What prejudices do you have regarding race, religion, gender, class, or other qualities that would make it a challenge for you to look at all men and women as your brothers and sisters? Be honest. Can you overcome these biases through this new understanding?

Repeat this affirmation when needed to overcome prejudice:

We are one human family. All men and women are my brothers and sisters under God.

IN HEAVEN

Where does our father reside? And why is this emphasized in the prayer?

This element of the Lord's Prayer is our constant reminder that you have chosen to be on earth, while God remains in heaven to guide you on your path. Heaven is a place of spiritual purity and perfection. It is what we strive for, while earth is a flawed and imperfect location. Heaven is where God resides and where the answers are, but earth is filled with unanswered questions.

> *You are on earth to learn.*
> *God is in heaven to teach.*
> *That is divine order.*

You are here because you have chosen to work through your lessons toward becoming a being of love in God's image while here on earth. It is the first part of the universal promise that we all made to our Father: to work toward perfecting our soul while living in harmony with, and in service to, the others who have done the same.

Like any loving parent, God wants only what is best for his children. In his efforts to teach and protect us, he sometimes makes the lessons hard, for that is the only way that we learn. Have you ever prayed for something you wanted with all your might yet still not received it? And later in your life—sometimes years later—you realized that there was a powerful reason that your prayer wasn't answered?

I am the mother of three boys, two of them teenagers. Now, I love them beyond words and want them to have everything they need and to be happy. However, I am also aware that they are adolescent boys, and often they will ask to do something that I don't feel is healthy or safe for them. I refuse their requests when I fear they may endanger themselves. What responsible parent wouldn't? We have to say no to our children to protect them. As a result of our age and experience, we most often know better than they do.

In the same way, most of us are spiritual adolescents before God, and he will refuse our requests if what we are asking for is not safe for us in the long run. He knows better than we do. And like teenagers, sometimes we will rail against that authority, angry and hurt that we didn't get what we asked for. I don't mean to sound condescending by referring to you as a spiritual adolescent, so please don't be offended. Believe me, I am one as well. Most of us who aren't enlightened masters fall into the spiritual adolescent category. And I've actually only ever met one person I truly felt to be an enlightened master. Of course, we've all likely encountered people who claim to be, but that's another story.

The Gospel of Philip addresses this question in a particularly illustrative and clear way:

> *What belongs to the father belongs to the son,*
> *but while he is still young, he is not entrusted with all that is his.*
> *When he is mature, his father gives it to him.*

Further to this idea of parenting, what do we do with our children when they misbehave? We often ground them. Think about that term for a moment. "You're grounded!" Grounding is a good thing that keeps our feet firmly on the earth when we most need them to be. It is a strong tool to make us think about what we have done wrong. Often when an obstacle is thrown into our path, it is God grounding us. He is not "punishing us" in the way that the Old Testament God did. This is not a God to be feared. Rather he is gently but firmly providing us with lessons that will keep us on our path, lessons that will help us to stay *grounded*. This is a God to be loved. He is behaving as what he is, our Father, and he resides in the perfect place we all aspire to share with him: heaven.

There is some more very good news here. The more you pray and become aligned with God, the fewer the disappointments and the shorter the learning curve! When you are living in harmony with your higher purpose, you will not encounter the force of external resistance the way you would otherwise. This is the beginning of bringing heaven to earth.

MAY YOUR NAME BE HALLOWED

Hallowed means holy, and these words are our reminder that the name of God is sacred in a new and exciting way. This is not simply a warning about "not taking the Lord's name in vain," although that commandment is far from trivial. Instead, this line means that each and every time you invoke God's love and presence into your daily living, you are creating a sacred space in which to live. Your words are powerful and each has meaning, so when you speak of God, do it with love!

But the sanctity of God's name lies not only in the invoking of it but in what it contains, which is *essence*. The essence of God is omniscient, all-knowing. He sees all that we do not see and knows all that we do not know. This is a cornerstone of faith, for it is within this understanding that we are able to accept completely that God will make parental decisions that are in our best interest as his beloved child: he always knows best because he sees the big picture that is life and creation.

But as any parent of multiple children can tell you, sometimes decisions have to be made where the needs of the many outweigh the desires of the one. All God's children must be loved and considered equally.

Sometimes we cannot know or understand why we are denied something we want so badly because we cannot see the entire scope of what God sees and the impact our wishes may have on someone else. We cannot always grasp the enormity of divine will and the part we play within it. But each of us does indeed play a unique and critical part in God's plan, and understanding what that role is will solidify the foundation of your spiritual and physical future.

By invoking God's hallowed name, we are also creating a sacred space in which to pray. This line ends our invocation to God and creates the setting for the rest of the prayer, where we reaffirm our commitment to him while requesting that he listen to us.

THE SECRET OF LIFE

"Keep the oaths that you have made to the Lord."
Matthew 5:33

The path of the first petal asks you to examine all the complexities that come with the word *faith*: faith in God, faith in each other as God's children, and the element that we will address now, faith in yourself. When I share this process with others, I find over and over that this is the element that most pilgrims struggle with.

Here and now, you must accept a spiritual concept as instrumental to your faith in order to proceed any further. *Here is the true secret of life.* Ready?

*Y*ou made a promise to God to carry out a specific set of duties and to accomplish a predetermined mission during your life on earth.

How and if you do that is up to your own free will, but your understanding and fulfillment of that promise and mission is the key factor in determining your happiness, fulfillment, and abundance.

Go back and reread that as many times as you need to, because it is this understanding that will transform you above anything else.

You are special. You are unique. You chose to come here to do something that only you can do, something that you and God agreed to together.

Now, what is it?

I find that there are two types of students on this path: those who know exactly what they are here to do and those who have absolutely no idea. There is very little gray area. If you are one of those who know exactly why you are here and what you are here to do, congratulations! You are one step closer to achieving absolute fulfillment. But I urge you to complete the exercises here anyway, to see if they take you to new and higher levels of understanding.

For those of you who are unsure what your purpose is, which is likely the majority, you can begin exploring this critical question about your own destiny in very simple ways. Start with your greatest dreams and aspirations. They are your signposts.

Your dreams are not accidental, they are not random.
What you dream of doing is your soul's way of reminding you
of what you are here to do to fulfill your promise to God.

Often the clues to your mission in life come in early childhood. Maybe you always loved to sing or were a natural leader or were really great at science. Maybe you are the person whom everyone comes to for advice, or someone who has an amazing affinity with animals or works really well with kids. Maybe you are exceptionally detail-oriented or love to read. *What you are good at and what you love to do are clues to your destiny.* Destiny means *to determine.* The set of tools and talents that you brought with you were *predetermined* to give you everything you need to succeed in your mission. They are part of your destiny.

As an example from my own life, I knew that I wanted to write from the time I was in the third grade. I came from a boisterous Irish family, and my grandparents would come back from trips to Ireland with beautiful photographs that inspired my imagination. I dreamed of going to visit my ancestral homeland every day, but as I could not, I wrote a short story about a little girl who found a magical way to visit any place in the world she wanted to see. My third grade teacher, Mrs. Margucci, recognized something in the writing, and her subsequent actions shaped my life (there is a special place in heaven for teachers). She read the story out loud to the class and then called my mother to tell her she thought I had writing talent that should be encouraged. From that day to this, I knew I wanted to be a writer and never stopped dreaming about what that could be like. Not only did I enjoy the process of creating the story, but I loved sharing it with my peers and my parents. These were clues to the promise I made before incarnation, signposts to my destiny. This is what I *wanted* to do because it was what I was *here to do*. It was my *reason for being*.

As I began to work through the path of the rose with six petals in my own spiritual education much later in life, I had to understand how my aspirations to be a writer were related directly to the promise I made to God. I discovered through prayer and life experience that my own promise was to retrieve stories and teachings from history that had been nearly lost, to honor brave and inspirational people who changed the world but were somehow forgotten in the telling of the great human story. My promise was to resurrect the collective wisdom and legacies of the past and then create books intended to entertain, educate, and inspire others for the future. Once I aligned myself with that promise, embraced it fully and understood it, my career as a writer flourished and the cycle of miracles began in earnest. And writing, always a great joy to me, became an absolutely euphoric experience.

To help you discover your own promise, later in this chapter I suggest a blue-sky exercise where anything is possible, so dream as broadly as your heart and mind will let you. *Do not limit yourself*. If your greatest desire in life is to travel all over the world, then perhaps that is exactly what you should be doing. There are careers that allow you to do that and pay you for it. I have one. Remember my story from the third grade? I wrote it originally because I wanted to travel to Ireland and was unable to do so. My desire to travel became an obsession as I got older, but this was also a signpost that pointed directly to my life's mission. I needed to travel constantly to collect all the stories that I promised to tell. Therefore, my dream of traveling the world was not a random or frivolous desire. It pointed me in the direction of a tool that would prove necessary to carry out my mission. Someone who does not love to travel extensively, who hates to fly, or does not want to interact with unfamiliar cultures regularly would not love my job, but for me it is pure bliss.

So don't edit yourself. Dare to dream, and dream big. It is what you have come here to do.

And remember that it is never too late to follow your own bliss. So many times I have heard someone say, "But I'm too old to change my life now." Rubbish. Eliminate that thought as fast as you can. You are never too old to find your faith and to experience pure joy. Never. Equally, there is no such thing as wasted time. So while we are tossing all our outmoded beliefs in the trash, get rid of regrets for all the things you did not do. Not one minute of your life has been wasted because each experience you have had brings you to this very moment as the person you are today. All of it matters. Bless your past for the lessons you have learned so that you may seize your future.

TAKE THE LEAP OF FAITH INTO YOUR TRUE DESTINY

As for the present, if you are currently immersed in a career or life path that makes you miserable in any way, you are in the wrong place and you are not on the path to fulfilling your promise. You need to take action to change that.

Here is a crucial spiritual truth to meditate upon:

> *Fulfilling your promise will never make you unhappy.*
> *Living your destiny can only bring you joy.*

Your destiny may bring you challenges along the way, but it will always bring you happiness, and you will be regularly rewarded for carrying out the tasks necessary in fulfilling your promise.

Think in terms of a job interview followed by successful long-term employment. When you apply for a job, there should be a specific job description. In the interview, your prospective boss lays out the duties, and you agree to do them, all the while emphasizing why you are the person best suited for the available position. You get hired and you go to work. When you are an outstanding employee and carry out all the duties that you were hired for and get along beautifully with your co-workers, the boss is happy. If you are working for a benevolent and fair employer, you are rewarded with raises, promotions, and bonuses. A good boss wants you to have whatever you need to feel secure and satisfied so that you will continue to carry out your duties with absolute commitment and conscientiousness.

See where this is going? In this case, *life is your job and God is your boss*. When you are carrying out the tasks you agreed upon, everyone is happy. When you are immersed in other roles and activities that are not related to your specific job description, you will need to face the boss and learn how to redirect your energies.

I know a lot of people who are immersed in careers that they never wanted because someone else—usually a parent or spouse—thinks it's a good idea. It's stable, it has benefits, it is what they are "supposed" to do. Often people stay in a career because they invested years in their education, only to discover that they are dreadfully unhappy in the profession they trained for. I worked for years in high-pressure jobs with an entertainment conglomerate, in corporate positions that made it very difficult for me to find the time to write or explore my creativity or spirituality. During the last two years of that work, I suffered from debilitating migraines. No treatment, no medication, no doctor was able to save me from them. Through my spiritual practice, I came to the realization that I would have these headaches for as long as I stayed in a job that was counterproductive to my life's mission. Although abandoning such steady and well-paying work to pursue my creative goals and fulfill my spiritual promises was terrifying at first, it was the best life choice I have ever made. And I have not experienced a single migraine from that day to this.

There is another critical message here for all couples who are in a committed relationship: your faith must extend to your partner. You must support your partner's destiny with the same passion with which you pursue your own. The message is similar for parents. Support your children in every way you can while allowing them to be themselves. While we all want our children to be successful and stable, it is vital that we don't prevent them from finding their destinies by pushing them into lives that they will never find fulfilling. I know several middle-aged lawyers, doctors, and engineers who are miserable because they entered into these careers solely to make their parents happy.

It takes courage to change your path in midlife, either personally or professionally, unless you are aligned with your destiny. Once you take a vow to keep your promise to God, doors will open up that were previously shut tight or even invisible. It is a literally miraculous process, and one that has to be experienced to be fully appreciated and believed. I am willing to bet that many of you reading right now have been thinking about making a life change. Sometimes God taps us on the shoulder very gently, and for quite a long time, to let us know that it is time to move forward. However, when we ignore that gentle hint, sometimes God becomes a little more forceful. Or as I explain it most simply to my friends, "When you ignore the tapping, sometimes God hits you with a two-by-four across the head." Years ago when I first started sharing this idea, I went out and purchased two-by-fours at a lumber company for my friends and wrote their names on them. We were all attempting to make major life and career changes at the time that were challenging and often difficult. We were committed to helping each other. The idea for the two-by-four was to keep the board in a prominent place so that every time any of us was deviating from our spiritual path, we would be reminded of the risks. We had fun with it, and it helped all of us to stay on track and work together to support each other when challenged.

Just as all good parents would rather reward their children than punish them, so would God prefer to lavish you with joyous opportunities, rather than see you suffer in unhappiness or illness. The choice, quite simply, is your own.

It is human nature to wait for a safety net to appear before taking a death-defying leap. We spend our lives working hard, saving what little we can, hoping that one day we may be secure enough to go out and do "what we really want to do." Unfortunately, this plan rarely works because it is not in harmony with spiritual law. Virgil wrote, "Fortune favors the bold." I would paraphrase the great poet in more spiritual terms by saying *God favors those who have the courage to fulfill their promise.* It is, in fact, the energy of jumping—the proverbial leap of faith— that actually creates the safety net. At first this appears to be a spiritual catch-22, but in reality it is a test of our strength and our faith in our own divine promise. Great achievement often requires great risk, and yet that risk is transformed into safety when we are in harmony with our destiny.

One of my favorite films is the third in the Indiana Jones series, *Indiana Jones and the Last Crusade.* The tests that our hero, Indy, must pass in order to reach the Holy Grail are all symbolic of our own human quests. There is a scene where Indiana Jones must make a leap of faith; he must jump from a precipice with nothing but the belief that he will not fall to his death. As he takes the first, potentially fatal, step off the cliff, a previously invisible bridge appears that carries him safely to his destiny. I always cheer this scene out loud when I watch it, as it illustrates perfectly this concept of having the courage to follow our faith.

Please remember this is an *allegory* and Indiana Jones is a *movie*. Do not go jumping off real cliffs. And don't laugh, either. I really do have to say that because some people take spiritual learning very literally. But the point is that somewhere along the way, we have turned everything upside down! We have fallen into a trap of spending the majority of our lives immersed in drudgery that doesn't make us happy or fulfilled. It isn't supposed to be that way. We are here to *live*, not just *survive*. Our Father wants his children to be happy, and he will nudge you if he sees that you are on the wrong path, if you are on a path that cannot bring you joy. If God sees that you recognize his nudging and yet still ignore it, he will often become more forceful.

There is a quote from an ancient Gnostic text that I think illustrates this concept particularly well, and shows us that our earliest Christian brethren grasped this idea fully. It reads:

The Father does not sow fear, but pours forth persuasion.
Echoes from the Gnosis

I was discussing this notion recently on a pilgrimage in France with a wise friend of mine named Claire, who, as a psychologist and life coach, has learned a lot about human behavior. She summed up this idea—that God will urge you to find your correct path as fiercely as becomes necessary, particularly if he sees that you are ignoring his message—with a very simple yet powerful statement:

*J*ump. *Or be pushed.*

Exercise: **Why Are You Here?**

- Do you have a specific talent or skill that stands out? Is there something that people tell you that you are particularly good at? Write down what those things are and how they make you feel about yourself. This is not strictly occupational. It can be any quality that you possess that can be used for good.

- Do you have a great passion for certain activities? Sports, music, travel, computers? Write in detail about anything that applies, and write about ways that they can become a career path or life choice for you. Again, do not impose limits on yourself by being "realistic." Divine intelligence is far more creative than we can imagine. Focus on what the career and life path would look like, not the steps that you would need to take to make that happen. Let God handle those details for now.

- What does your perfect life look like? Describe what one perfect day, from waking up in the morning to going to bed at night, would look like for you in your ideal, happiest life.

- Is there something holding you back from pursuing a life goal that you know would bring you more happiness? What is the obstacle? Sometimes simply recognizing the obstacle is the most important step to removing it. For example, if you want to be an artist but you can't leave a job that has medical benefits, don't make the assumption that you can't have both! God is infinitely more creative about granting your heart's desire than you can even imagine. This truth will be discussed in greater detail in the chapter on petal four, abundance.

Here is one quick hint to help you understand what your own mission is:

> *All of us, each and every human being alive,*
> *made a promise to create the kingdom of heaven on earth*
> *as a part of our path.*
> *That promise is universal, it belongs to each of us.*

This faith provides you with a place to start. It may take you some time to discover exactly where everything else fits in, but you can begin by crafting a mission statement based in the understanding that you are here to make a positive contribution to the human family.

Exercise: **Your Mission Statement**

- How can you take an activity that you love and use it in some way that benefits others? It can be educational, entertaining, or inspirational, but there must be some way in which it will better the planet or help other people. It can be something that makes you financially so successful that it allows you to fund charitable projects and be a philanthropist, or an interpersonal or emotional strength that gives you a special ability to work with others. Write about the possibilities.

- How do the answers to all the above questions begin to help you understand what your own mission is? In other words, what promise did you make to God about your life? Allow yourself time to meditate and pray on this question each day if the answer still feels distant and elusive to you. Ask God to help you remember your promise. The answer can come in amazing ways.

- If you are still not sure why you are here and what your promise was, *that's okay.* But at this stage you must be able to acknowledge that you have a mission and a destiny and that you are open to being shown just what that is. For now, simply affirm that you are here to do something. Reinforce your understanding that you are part of the divine plan and that your contribution matters, that you believe you bring to the world your own unique set of experiences and skills and are valuable. This is the essence of *faith in yourself.*

Repeat this affirmation as needed:

I have a unique destiny and every day that path is being revealed to me in new ways.

- Write your mission statement. It should contain the reason that you are here, the nature of your promise to God, and how you intend to carry it out. Each mission statement is personal and unique, but all should include an affirmation of what you are here to do and your unshakable commitment to fulfill that mission as a part of God's plan. If you are still struggling with this, write the above affirmation and continue to use it in your daily prayer, repeating it as often as you need to.
- Realize that you can edit or amend your mission statement at any time. The more you pray, the more clarity you will have in your mission. So expect it to change, and allow it to. This will also help you eliminate the fear of "getting it wrong." Don't worry about any of that. Just get started, and allow it to evolve along with your own spiritual understanding.

The path of the first petal is *faith*, and it is the foundation upon which your spiritual life is built. One of my favorite quotes comes from Gandhi, who said, "Be the change you wish to see in this world." I would add to that, if I may be so bold, "And be the change you wish to see in your life." Live your mission statement, and be conscious every single day about keeping your promise to God. When you are confronted with decisions or dilemmas regarding your career and life path, your first question should always be, "Which choice is the most harmonious with my mission?" When you act within that guideline, you will make the right choices.

Now that you have explored your relationship with God and have acknowledged the exciting aspects of your unique destiny in the world, you are ready to move forward into the next petal of the rose: surrender. This next one is a tad tricky, but mastery of it will bring you more spiritual freedom and peace of mind than you ever dreamed possible. I'll let you in on a secret: it's my favorite petal of the rose, and I'm not sure how I ever lived without it.

"Therefore I tell you, do not worry about your life. . . .
Look at the birds of the air.
They do not reap or sow and yet your heavenly Father feeds them.
Are you not much more valuable than they?
Who of you by worrying can add a single hour to your life?
Your heavenly Father knows what you need. . . .
Seek his kingdom and his righteousness and
all things will be given to you. . . .
Therefore do not worry about tomorrow,
for tomorrow will worry about itself."

Matthew 6:25–34

VI

The Second Petal—Surrender

Surrender

*T*he second petal of the rose corresponds to these words of the prayer:

> *May your kingdom come,*
> *may your will be done*

These two lines of the prayer are your promise to create heaven on earth. Every time you recite the words *your kingdom come*, you are committing to make the world a better place. *Your will be done* are the words that will help you to surrender your more ego-driven desires to follow the destiny that God has planned for you.

GOD IS BETTER AT THIS THAN YOU ARE

Thus there are two steps toward surrender to be taken along the path of the second petal. The first, and most difficult, is to surrender to the divine will. Once you have accepted that before your birth you made a promise to fulfill a unique purpose in God's plan, you must surrender to that idea and surrender completely. Most people have an aversion to words like *surrender* and *obedience*, yet when they apply to your relationship with God, they become the most liberating words in our language. It is in the act of surrendering to your role in a divine plan that you will find true inner peace.

The steps you take in your life either help you keep your promise to God or they do not. When everything falls into place and life runs smoothly, you are on the right path. When you encounter obstacles and everything seems to be an uphill battle, it is usually an indication that you are out of alignment with your spiritual purpose and need to do some adjusting.

During difficult or challenging times, when things really seem to be going wrong or at least not as planned, embrace the affirmation:

Y*our will, not my will, be done.*

Say it out loud and say it often. You will be pleasantly surprised just how quickly this simple chant can alter your reality when you speak it from the heart. If something that you really desired does not come to pass, repeat these words and focus hard on their meaning. If your desire wasn't fulfilled, it wasn't supposed to be. Your particular wish was counterproductive to God's plan, although it may be difficult for you to understand why. But comprehending this truth and accepting it with all your heart and spirit will not only make you feel better, it will open the door for God to provide you with a better, greater opportunity to erase any residual disappointment.

These sacred words work when you are truly committed to their meaning. If you don't see a shift in your circumstances quickly, move to the next level in your prayer process by affirming to God:

I am certain that I am experiencing this pain / hardship / challenge because there is a lesson for me in this which will advance my spiritual learning. I surrender to your ultimate wisdom and pray that you will help me to grasp the lesson quickly so that I may move on with my life in your service!

I have never seen these affirmations fail when used in absolute sincerity. Never. In fact, I have seen very literal miracles wrought where these words were spoken, including in the NICU when my son was given a death sentence. These words of surrender contain secrets of the universe. Don't be afraid to use them. When God sees that you are earnest about doing the right thing, he will provide for you by offering a brighter path. This is the beginning of the cycle of miracles. It works, and it is beautiful to behold as it does.

There is an old adage that God has three answers to all prayer requests. They are

Yes.

Yes, but in my time.

No, but only because I have something much better planned for you.

When I first began to learn this process, I chanted *Your will, not my will, be done* over and over every time I was feeling emotionally or spiritually challenged—which was about fifty times a day. Okay, that's possibly an exaggeration, but not really a large one. It takes time and effort for most of us to overcome our natural, egocentric thinking that everything that happens in our day is really all about us all the time. But how often have your best-laid plans not played out exactly as you had envisioned? It happened because your plans and God's plans were not the same. (There is another reason that involves the free will of your brother and sister humans, which will be discussed at length later.)

Guess what? God always wins. When our plans go awry, we are challenged to surrender: surrender to the understanding that the divine will is beyond our understanding.

I fought surrender harder than any other aspect of the teachings, yet I have learned to love it more than any other. It is the cornerstone of my faith, and it has brought me through some very dark nights of the soul. This practice of surrender, more than any other element of my spiritual training, transformed me. It brought me inner peace when I feared I would never know the meaning of those words, and I do mean never. Now when I am restless with anxiety, I know it is time to get on my knees in the second petal of the rose and surrender it all to God. Surrender takes work, it takes repetition to live it every day, and sometimes it eludes us even when we should know better.

We are not the architects of this glorious world we are building. God is. We are the laborers, and each of us has a specific job to carry out. Some of us try too hard to control all the details in the master plan, when the only thing that is expected, required, or desired of us is to do our individual jobs, and do them with love. Surrender the details. Let God design the world. It's not for you to do.

The surrender affirmations have become an integral part of my daily practice, and in fact when I wake up in the morning, I start my day by saying this:

> God, *I am turning this day over to you. Your will, not my will, be done. Please guide me to do the right thing and to stay on my path in your service, and to do so with love.*

I find that to be healthy, preventive spiritual medicine. When I start each day with this prayer, I very rarely need to use the other "rescue remedy" affirmations. I often say the Prayer of Saint Francis of Assisi as a spiritual supplement, and I keep a copy of it on my computer and even in my bathroom to be sure I don't miss it. For whereas Jesus was giving us the key to the secrets of the universe, Francis, walking in his footsteps, gave us the key to right conduct with our brothers and sisters on earth. You will find his prayer, and others, in the back of this book to help support your spiritual progress.

I have found that there is a remarkable freedom that comes with realizing that life isn't all about you! Try it. You'll never go back.

THE PARABLE OF THE FARMER AND THE COW

There was once a farmer who lived a very simple yet happy life, with his wife of fifty years, who had been his childhood sweetheart. His wife was a delicate thing, fine-boned and of a sensitive constitution, but she was a hard worker all the same. Together, they built a little farm where they grew a few crops. But the source of their livelihood was a special cow who gave an abundance of sweet milk. It was the most sought-after milk in the county, and the farmer and his wife were able to support themselves quite comfortably from this single cow. In addition to her ability to produce a great abundance of milk, the cow was also of a sweet disposition and had become a cherished pet.

The farmer was a simple man and pious. Each night before he went to bed, for fifty years, he prayed over the one thing that always worried him: "Dear God, please keep my beautiful little wife safe and healthy." And God, hearing a prayer full of love and selflessness, did just that. Every day.

The farmer and his wife lived in harmony until one difficult season when a majority of the crops were damaged by blight. Most of the neighboring farms were wiped out, but this couple were able to survive because of their prize cow. Then one terrible morning, the farmer awoke to silence. This was strange, because the cow usually began crying to be milked early in the morning. Fearing something may have happened to their prize pet, the farmer ran to the barn. He could not believe his eyes as he looked at the sight that waited in the straw.

Their wonderful cow was dead.

He ran in and told his wife, and they held each other and cried for a long while. They loved the cow and would miss her, but they had to immediately consider the financial impact of this loss. The milk from this cow was their sole source of income since the crops had failed.

The farmer was at a loss, so he walked to the village church and got down on his knees to pray.

"Dear Lord, I am an honest man and simple, and I have always been of great faith. Why have you punished me in this way? Why, Lord? Why?"

There was silence for a moment, but then the farmer heard a voice boom through the little church.

"I have not punished you," said the voice of the Lord. "I have answered your prayer, the same prayer you have said each night for fifty years."

The farmer was puzzled. "But how? I do not understand."

The voice of God continued. "Each night you pray for the health of your beloved wife."

"Yes, I do."

"And yesterday your wife was going to search through the fields to see if there were any vegetables left that had not been rotted by the blight. You discussed this with her. Do you remember?"

"Yes, I do."

"Well, there were radishes left in the far field that she would have found. But the radishes were poisonous, although you would not have known it to look at them. Your constitution is strong, but hers is delicate. The radishes would have killed her for sure.

"So instead of allowing her to find them, I had the cow break out of the barn and wander off into the far field. The cow ate all the blighted radishes, so that your wife would be spared."

The farmer cried as the light of God filled him and the church. The Lord had, indeed, answered his prayers. His wife was safe and healthy, in spite of their heartache over the loss of the cow. He surrendered to the loss graciously and stayed on his knees and thanked God for watching over them and prayed that God would continue to do so, if such was his will.

God rewarded the farmer and his wife for their faith. Their crops returned the next season in an abundance never before seen, and they were able to purchase a pair of new cows, both of whom gave award-winning sweet milk. And the farmer's little wife remained safe and healthy throughout a very long life, filled with love and faith.

I do not know what the origins of this story are, as I have heard it over many years in different forms and from different sources. I first heard a version of it in Ireland when I was a teenager, so I have always assumed that its origins lay in the rich storytelling lands of my ancestors.

In my family, we refer to this parable a lot. It has led to a philosophy that we refer to as "taking the cow." When something negative happens to us that does not involve physical harm to anyone we love, we surrender to it in the same way that the farmer does in the story. We look at each other and say, "He took the cow," and then thank God for protecting our family and keeping us safe, trusting that there must be a reason for the hardship in the greater plan of divine will. The strange thing about this kind of surrender is that the purpose of such adversity most often does explain itself with time. You may not understand why some unfortunate event has befallen you at the moment it occurs, but time will usually reveal the reason if you are patient.

My clever and faith-full Irish friend, who has an amazing knack of simplifying the most complex theories into bite-size pieces that everyone can ingest, summarizes the issue of surrender this way:

> *If you truly believe everything happens for a reason,*
> *you will never have a bad day.*

Really, it's that simple.

I have seen over and over that God answers our prayers, but I have also seen that the answer rarely comes in the form that we expect! Learning to trust the unexpected, even to welcome it, has been the most transformational lesson in my life, just as it was for the farmer in the parable. How could I have ever known that the answer to my creative prayer—how to portray Jesus well and correctly in my book, and how to write about the miracles appropriately—would come to me through seeing my son through a life-threatening illness? Could I have grasped the essence of miracles if I had not been through that particular hardship? I really don't think so. The answer to my prayer had to be that visceral, that personal, that extreme. And God knew it.

The person I had once been was shattered during Shane's illness. The person I am now emerged, new and whole, from that experience.

This is my experience of what Jesus refers to when he speaks of being born again in the Gospel of John (3:7, 21):

> "You should not be surprised at my saying, 'You must be born again.' . . . whoever lives by the truth comes into the light, so that it may be seen plainly that what he has done has been done through God."

Exercise: **Surrendering to Divine Will**

Think about a time when you did not receive something that you wanted badly yet realized later that it was for the best. The disappointment can involve anything: a relationship, a job, an opportunity. Answer these questions about the circumstances:

- What did you want and why did you want it? What did you think it would do for your life at the time that you wanted it?

- Why didn't it happen, and how did your understanding of why it didn't occur change over time? Were you angry at first? Depressed?

- How long did it take for you to realize that you were denied this wish for your own highest good? Days, weeks, years? Or are you still wrestling with it? If so, apply the affirmations given earlier in this section, and see if they help you to move through any residual pain or resentment you have.

SURRENDER YOUR WORRIES

The second step toward surrender is to turn your worries and fears over to God, who is far more able to cope with them than you are. Your reward for surrendering to God's will is the greater gift of also surrendering your pain. When you align yourself with the idea that everything is happening according to a divine plan, your anxieties will be instantly reduced.

One of my personal failings has always been my need to worry. I'm a huge worrier. Worrying has probably taken years off my life, destroyed my stomach lining, and generally done me no good. I realize now that worry is spiritually and emotionally detrimental. It also indicates lack of faith. It needs to be surrendered.

I have struggled with this issue for years. I still do. But while I was learning this prayer process, I had a very vivid and beautiful dream about Jesus that helped me to surrender my worry. I will share it with you here, as it has proven effective over and over again for many people.

THE DREAM OF JESUS AND
THE WHITE SACK OF SORROWS

I was having a very hard time. Everything was a challenge, and I had more to worry about than I could possibly handle. I cried myself to sleep that night, not sure how I was going to get through the next day, much less the next week, month, or year.

I began to dream, and my tears came with me from my waking into my sleep. My dreams have always been clear and vivid, and this one was no different. I was sitting on the bank of a river, one that flowed through a lush, verdant landscape. I think it was Wales or some other richly

Celtic locale that speaks to my soul, as I dream about such places often. And yet I continued to cry, despite my presence in such a beautiful place. And then I heard a voice behind me, rich and resonant, ask, "Why are you crying?"

I looked around; standing there, perfect and luminous, was Jesus.

"Come, walk with me." He gestured. "I want to show you something." I followed him and we walked along the river. I wiped my eyes as he asked me again why I was weeping when the world around me was so lovely and blessed by God. I told him that I was tired and overwhelmed and didn't know how I was going to pay the mortgage next week and a number of other worrisome things that fell from my mouth as we walked. He was silent, listening, as he led me to an ancient oak tree on the riverbank. Hanging from one of the branches was a large sack made of a pristine white fabric. Jesus walked to the branch and untied the rope that attached the sack to the tree. He held the bag open and out toward me.

"This is the Sack of Sorrows. I want you to put everything that is currently troubling you into this bag. Get it out of your brain and your body, and pour it all into this sack. Just speak all your worries into it now, until you have none left."

I am not one to argue with the savior of the world. Besides, it sounded like a lovely idea. And so I took the bag and cried all my worries into it until I was completely exhausted with the effort.

"Finished?" Jesus asked. I nodded mutely in reply as he tied the rope tight around the white sack before turning to hurl it into the river.

"See that? That is the river of time and it flows directly to God. Now, he will take all these worries away from you so they do not burden you any longer. But you must release them. Watch them bob down the river, and then just let them go . . ."

This I did, already feeling amazingly lighter. Before he left, Jesus turned to me and said, "You can come here anytime, and here you will find the White Sack of Sorrows hanging from this tree. When your worries become too much, put them in this bag and send them to God. Oh, and tell your friends that they can come here too. The sack's capacity is unlimited, just as God is."

Then he was simply gone. I have noticed that Jesus has a funny way of coming and going as he pleases. And he never uses doors.

When I woke from that dream, I felt infinitely better. And I had hope, where there had previously been none. That hope translated into physical miracles. Over the next few days, the primary issues that had kept me awake and in tears were resolved in ways I had never dreamed. Money arrived unexpectedly, as did additional opportunity. God really had taken my worries away from me.

I find that people respond one of two ways to this dream. They either embrace it, try it, and benefit greatly, or they shy away from it completely. I have shared this dream with many friends and invited them to use this same visualization when they are feeling overwhelmed by worry. Those who use it see astonishing results. I have also met many people who were afraid to have any kind of direct interaction with God because they felt that it might be "against their religion," that only an intermediary cleric was supposed to intervene on their behalf. There are a lot of people who feel that they are not allowed to have a personal and direct experience with Jesus or with God, because some religious authority, or parent quoting a religious authority, gave them that idea. But you *are*. You are supposed to have both. And don't just take my word for it. Jesus says it repeatedly in the Bible. After insisting that we pray directly to God, in the privacy of our own room (and not in a church, and not in the presence of a cleric—this is just between you and God), Jesus gets a little impatient with us for being so slow to catch on, as illustrated in the Gospel of Luke, chapter 6, verses 46–49:

> "Why do you call on me, 'Lord, Lord,' and do not do what I say? I will show you what he is like who comes to me and hears my words and puts them into practice. He is like a man building a house, who dug down deep and laid the foundation on a rock. When a flood came, the torrent struck that house but could not shake it, because it was well built. But the one who hears my words and does not put them into practice is like a man who built his house on the ground without a foundation. The moment the torrent struck that house, it collapsed and its destruction was complete."

Direct access to God and authentic mystical experience—without a middleman—make up the foundation of which Jesus speaks. He entreats us to talk to God directly, and through the Lord's Prayer he shows us how to do that. His emphasis is on making us whole as individuals, fully realized, with direct and unimpeded access to God.

Still other people feel that they are somehow "not worthy" of direct access to God. They believe, perhaps, that mysticism and miracles are reserved for saints and are the domain of the holy, but this is simply not true. Jesus again makes this point clear in the Gospel of John, chapter 14, verse 12:

> "I tell you the truth. The person that believes in me will do the same things I have done. Yes! He will do even greater things than I have done."

Exercise: **Surrender Self-Doubt and Claim Your Worthiness**

- Do you have any issues of "worthiness" about God? Do you feel that you are not worthy to have a direct relationship with God for any reason?
- Do you believe that you can have mystical experiences, such as dreams or visions of the divine, as part of the natural course of your spirituality? If not, why not?
- Recently on a daytime talk show, an atheist guest told a Christian host that she was "crazy" because she admitted to talking to God on a regular basis. But in fact, everyone who prays talks to God and often hears a reply, in one form or another. Do you have any fear that people may think you are in any way unbalanced if you talk to God?

Use this affirmation as needed:

I am worthy of my healthy, direct relationship with God, and I surrender all my doubt about this.

One of my favorite Christian quotes comes from the brilliant and infinitely inspirational Gospel of Philip:

No one hides a thing of great value in a vase which is too visible. Treasures are hidden in inconspicuous pots.

And that, for me, is an accurate description of every one of us. We are a world full of treasures locked up inside these inconspicuous pots we call our bodies.

Once you have cleared the way to direct access to God and his miracles, I invite you to list all your worries and throw them into the white sack of sorrows. Visualize them floating down the river on their way to God, and really allow yourself to release them. Let them all go! Finally, if you are still feeling like you haven't completely surrendered your fears, pain, or woes, meditate at length on the passage about worry from the Gospel of Matthew that opened this section.

"Therefore I tell you, do not worry about your life!"

Now that you're feeling so much lighter, we can move to petal three, the path of service, and share our good fortune with the world!

"Give to the one who asks you,
and do not turn away
from the one who wants to borrow from you."

Matthew 5:42

VII

The Third Petal—Service

Service

*T*he *third petal* of the rose corresponds to these words of the prayer:

As in heaven, so upon earth.

God is all good, all the time.

I use that affirmation when good things happen; I use that affirmation when bad things happen. Because it is important to remember it. Every day.

It is a little too easy to blame God when something goes terribly wrong. I have known some truly decent people who struggled to believe in God because there is so much suffering in the world. They simply could not accept that a kind and just creator would allow some of the horrors that occur on our often troubled planet.

I used to be one of those people. When I first met my Catholic husband in Ireland many years ago, I shocked him on our first date by telling him that I was an atheist. And for a while, I did a good job of convincing myself that I was. What can I say? I was young, impressionable, and hopelessly naïve. I was also an aspiring writer and activist, living in Ireland during a very violent and troubled time. What I witnessed in the north of Ireland in the 1980s turned me against God for a while. The death, the suffering, the injustices—all were happening on God's watch and apparently in his name, and he wasn't doing a thing to intervene. I remember a line of poetry I wrote back then: "I no longer believe in God. I have seen too much of Belfast."

And so it was that I first blamed God for all the ills of a war that had lasted eight hundred years, before abandoning him completely.

But God hadn't abandoned *me*. Through the course of my life he continued to show himself to me, a little at a time, until I came back into the full understanding of divine presence and goodness in the world. I have since realized many things about wars, all wars, most significantly that they are caused and fought by human beings around issues of power, greed, and control.

So if the question is *Why doesn't God wipe out the evils of the world?* then the answer is *Because human beings created the evils of the world.* We must be accountable for our actions. God doesn't eradicate the human and environmental damage, because he didn't cause it. Mankind did. Therefore it is *our* responsibility to wipe out the evils of the world. God will help us to do it, but we must first show an understanding of our own failings that caused these problems, followed by our desire to set things to right.

Let's go back to the idea of parenting. When a child makes a terrible and destructive mess, what should a good parent do? Just clean it up quietly and let the child get away with it? Absolutely not. The child would learn nothing if he wasn't held accountable for his actions, and he would be therefore likely to make another mess. He would alienate his brothers and sisters and become decidedly hard to love if allowed to continue on such a destructive path. A good parent would insist that the child clean up the mess and make amends for any destruction he caused in the process. So it is with the world. God is waiting for us to clean up the mess we have made.

We have work to do.

CREATING HEAVEN

On the path of service in the third petal, you are asked to create heaven on earth through charitable actions. The greater our effort toward service, the faster we can and will clean up the mess. It is through *service* that we effect global transformation. Every single person who even makes a commitment to this idea makes a difference. Every act of goodness brings us a step closer to creating an earth that mirrors the perfection of heaven that God desires for us.

But sometimes the state of the world is so overwhelming that we get discouraged by the size and the weight of the problems. We are wrestling with enormous environmental issues, some of which we are told are irreparable; global poverty and starvation are widespread, seemingly endless wars rage around the world, disease is rampant, and the unspeakable horrors of genocide have been committed on two continents over the last fifteen years. Slavery is at its highest numbers in all of human history, with twenty-seven million people enslaved around the world. How could we have fallen so far? And how can we even begin to make improvements against so many devastating concerns? How can one individual impact on these worldwide catastrophes?

Yet in spite of the enormous odds, we really can save the world through our intention and our actions, one person at a time. Because here is another powerful element of divine law, one that I believe should be shared with every person who will listen:

> *Every good deed neutralizes a bad one.*
> *Every act of service eliminates an act of oppression.*
> *Every prayer for peace eradicates an impulse of war.*

Reread it as many times as you have to in order to make sure that it sticks. Memorize it, and spread the word. For this is truly the Good News.

Now imagine a hanging scale with one side representing the light in the world and one side representing the darkness. Good versus evil.

Every time you perform an act of kindness, service, or peace, you add to the "good" side of the scales. The more this happens, the deeper the scales dip toward the light of goodness in the world. Good outweighs bad with every single positive deed that occurs on earth. This is a world made up of energy, and we have the ability to impact on that energy for good or for ill. The choice is ours, and it is a choice we make with all our actions, every day.

Learn it and live it because it's the truth, the powerful truth that can and will save the world. Teach it to everyone who will listen. Start with your friends, your family, and especially your kids. Children are naturally pure and closest to God, and therefore they accept this concept instantly because they recognize it as the truth. The earlier this concept is taught, the better. We have to work hard on a planet of nearly seven billion souls, but we can do it. We need as many people as possible to commit to service and peace.

In fact, sharing this concept is an act of service!

Now, maybe you can't begin to even think about saving the whole world when you have enough of your own problems. Let me make this a little more personal by asking you to look at service in a way that hits closer to home. When you perform an act of kindness, service, or peace, you are creating your own spiritual insurance policy. Each positive deed that you perform raises the vibration of goodness and protection around you and your family and helps you attract more abundance into your life: abundance of wealth, abundance of love, abundance of well-being.

What you do makes a difference. What you think makes a difference. Who you are makes a difference, and every single person counts in this complex global equation. Never forget that. You and your actions matter, and they matter every day. So does the choice not to act.

Choosing to do nothing is the same as allowing evil to win. When we do nothing to help the world around us, we are allowing deposits on the side of evil to build up. This is why complacency is dangerous, not only to our souls but also to our planet. We will discuss this pitfall at greater length when we get to petal six, overcoming obstacles, as complacency is one of the seven deadly sins; it is one of the evils that we must be delivered from.

There are many ways to fulfill your service obligations, and good deeds come in many forms. Simply behaving in a kind and generous way toward everyone you meet is an act of service. Praying for someone is an act of service. *Every day you should choose at least one person to pray for. You should also pray for peace on earth.* Both of those efforts deposit "goodness" into the scales of light and darkness and therefore help you and help the world. Even on days when you are overworked, overwhelmed, and completely exhausted, you can still make your contribution to the world by simply saying a two-minute prayer for at least one person and the planet. Small as that may seem, it counts, and it matters.

Exercise: **Prayer as an Act of Service**

- Make a list of at least five people in your life whom you can pray for tonight. It can be for any reason. Perhaps someone you know is wrestling with illness, suffering from depression, or has just gone through a hard time. You can pray for your children, your partner, your parents, or your siblings, simply because you love them and want them to stay safe and happy.
- Write down a topic of world crisis that you feel moved by and can therefore pray about with some passion, for instance starvation or war. Just as a personal example, I pray every night for the end of slavery.
- Make a commitment to add these two elements of prayer—for individuals and the world—to your daily routine, either before you go to bed or when you wake up in the morning.

WHAT'S YOUR MOTIVATION?

Each act of service must be done out of a true sense of love, and not out of a sense of duty, in order to be successful. *Motive matters to God.* Jesus reminds us of this fact rather relentlessly as he tells us that God sees what we do in private and knows what thoughts motivate our actions. *Service must happen through love to count.* In fact, everything must happen through love to count. You can't give simply because you know you are obligated to. It is pointless to add points to your spiritual score-card so you will go to heaven, or to try to get service credits so you can then ask for whatever you want in the abundance arena. These acts fall into the same category as vain repetitions and what Jesus refers to as "hypocritical" church attendance for the sake of getting the acclaim for showing up.

Recently while traveling, my friend and I were going to view a particularly beautiful and famous church in Italy. Unbeknownst to us, a special mass was about to start, so many of the locals were in attendance. The ancient side door was sticky and hard to open, so while my friend struggled to get it open, an elderly woman behind us, desperate to get to the mass before it started, *began to hit him with her cane so that he would hurry!* Somewhere, the "love" piece of the Christian message just wasn't connecting with this lady. She was on a mission, but it was a mission of duty and obligation, not a mission of love and service.

Spend some time with this meditation from the Gospel of Philip:

> *Faith is receiving and love is giving.*
> *None can receive without faith,*
> *And none can give without love.*
> *When we believe, we are then capable of receiving.*
> *We give so that we may experience love.*
> *Whoever gives without love experiences nothing of importance.*

GOD GIVES TO THE GIVERS

The Gospel of Matthew tells us in chapter 19, verse 21:

> "If you want to be perfect, go sell your possessions and give to the poor, and you will have treasure in heaven."

This is a very important verse. I find that it scares people, who mis-interpret it as "sell *all* your possessions and give all your money away." Look closely. It doesn't say that. It says sell your possessions and give to the poor, but it doesn't say *all* of them. People think that abundance lies down one of two extreme and unlikely paths, neither of which is conducive to real inner peace or happiness. One path is recommended by the instant manifestation/consumer crowd who say you can snap your fingers and have anything you want. The other path is the way of the ascetic preachers who say you have to give away everything and abandon all connection to material concerns. Neither works. We have already discussed why the first process is flawed, but now let's look at the second.

We live in the material world and we must operate in it. In fact, we must operate in it effectively if we are going to make changes in the status of this planet. And we must feel comfortable and safe in our own lives and circumstances if we are going to focus on assisting others.

If you have ever been on an airplane, you know that as part of the safety instructions prior to takeoff, the flight attendants will demon-strate how oxygen masks will fall from the ceiling in the event of a drop in cabin pressure. What do they always tell you in the next sen-tence? Put your oxygen mask on first, before trying to help a child or other passenger that needs help. This is because you must be as stable as possible in order to help others!

The same is true of service. You have to be able to breathe on your own before you are stable enough to give aid to those around you. This is why giving everything away is not only unnecessary, it is actually counterproductive to the ultimate goal of service. The object here is to find balance. Give what you can, when you can. If you don't have money, give your time. If you don't have time, give your money. If you can, give both. Find the charity or cause that speaks to you, research it, and pledge to commit some aspect of yourself to that cause. I often recommend charities like Save the Children or Women for Women that operate on sponsorship programs. For a small monthly fee, usually about thirty dollars, you can change someone's life by providing them with access to food, health, education, or other vital services. Organizations like these are good options for busy people who want to see their money go to direct services and also want to have some personal contact with the people they are helping.

If money is really tight, you can volunteer to work at an animal shelter or to deliver meals to the infirm; the Salvation Army has many volunteer opportunities, as do many facilities for the homeless. You can give blood or sign up to be a bone marrow donor; both are actions that can save lives. Find ways that you can serve in your community when you can. Local libraries and hospitals often need people to read to children or to the blind. There are thousands of ways that you can serve. Find some. Even exerting the energy to search for an organization or cause to support is an act of service!

Exercise: **Finding Outlets for Service**

- What *global* cause or issue speaks to your heart and makes you want to effect change? If you could wave a magic wand right now and eradicate any ill in the world, what would it be? Now go out and research charities that serve that cause and see if any of them entice you to join them or give to them. If you are unable to do either, at least add that cause to your daily prayer schedule.

- What *local* cause in your community can you volunteer for or participate in? Are there local homeless shelters, animal rescue organizations, or programs for the elderly that require volunteers? Or donations? Donations don't have to be cash. Often shelters require canned food or blankets. In what ways can you be of service to your neighbors in your own community?

Think of the public figures who are extremely wealthy but also hugely philanthropic. A recent list of the most "charitable celebrities" appeared online, and the two at the top, not surprisingly, were Bill Gates and Oprah Winfrey. Now, most of you will immediately think, "But it's easy for them to give to charity. They're billionaires." But I would ask you to reverse that thinking, to consider that *they are billionaires because they are charitable.* God gave them opportunities toward increased prosperity because they lived lives of conscience and because he knew from their actions that they would change the world through their work. I urge you to look at the impact that the Bill and Melinda Gates Foundation has had on our suffering world and at the extraordinarily hands-on approach that Oprah Winfrey has in her humanitarian efforts. These are not people who give simply because charity is tax deductible. These are people who give because they care deeply about the world they live in. And the more they give, the more their empires appear to grow. It's quite a beautiful thing to watch, and a very valuable process to emulate.

Exercise: **Tithing to the Universe**

- In this exercise, choose one project or one circumstance that you would dearly love to see manifest in your life. Now attach a charitable commitment to it. In other words, make a promise to God. Say, "If it is your will and you help me to make this a reality, I will make the world a better place by contributing a percentage of its success to charity." You are promising that when what you are praying for manifests, you will give back to this particular cause. Your gift can be to a global or local charity, or even personal aid to a friend or family member, as long as it is given in the spirit of service and with love.

- Remember the example of Bill Gates and Oprah Winfrey, and think of ways that you can grow your own empire of giving. What would that look like for you? What charities would you support, or perhaps even create, if you had unlimited resources to do so?

It is always acceptable to "pray for something" when there is a service commitment attached to the request!

Always keep your promises, because I can assure you that God will keep his. Woe to those who promise charity and then do not deliver it after they have been given their heart's desire! You only get to violate an agreement with God once. Remember these wise words from Matthew:

> **"Freely you have received, freely give."**
> *Matthew 10:8*

The Gospel of Philip tells us that *humanity is the food of God*. In other words, every time that we behave in a humane way toward our brothers and sisters on earth, we are providing joy to our creator and nourishment to the divinity within ourselves.

BLESSED ARE THE PEACEMAKERS

There is perhaps no greater service that we can perform to demonstrate our love for God and our love for our neighbors than to work toward finding peaceful solutions to the world's conflicts. It is a global and human responsibility, an inseparable element of our promise to create heaven on earth; it is our mission, because heaven is, perhaps above all, a place of peace. When we say "As in heaven, so upon earth," we dedicate ourselves to making peace.

Bringing peace to a world submerged in conflict is an enormous challenge, but it is not impossible. Like everything else, it must be accomplished one step at a time and with all individuals doing what they can in their own lives to work toward that change. Praying for peace helps, and it helps immensely. Remember, every prayer for peace eradicates an impulse of war. In addition, our own behavior impacts the energy toward war or peace in our own lives, which are microcosms of the world around us. Do you act in a way that encourages conflict, or do you act in a way that encourages conflict resolution? Let's look.

Exercise: **Creating Peace in Your Own Life**

- Make a list of conflicts that have occurred in your personal life recently: arguments, disagreements, harsh words exchanged between you and another. Some of you won't have to look very far; others may have to reach back. FYI, this list includes Internet activity. Posting ugly messages behind false names creates conflict and is an act of aggression. Be honest, and list your transgressions. Go as far back as necessary to get a good accounting of where you have participated in or encouraged conflict.

- Look at the list and make another, of less aggressive ways you could have resolved or dealt with those circumstances. In any of these cases, could you have simply walked away and given the conflict no energy? Did you overreact in any of these circumstances? Did you feel bad or guilty later about yelling at someone or doing something that was hurtful or damaging to another? This is a clear indicator that you know in your heart and spirit that perpetuating the conflict was a mistake.

Use the following affirmation as needed when you are working through a conflict. I find that it is tremendously helpful in snapping me out of anger or aggression, because it reminds me that every conflict I participate in, no matter how small, impacts the energy of the world around me:

I will seek the most peaceful way to resolve this conflict for the sake of my own well-being and for the sake of the planet.

I am an outspoken woman, and that gets me into trouble sometimes, in public and in my own personal and spiritual development. I have opinions I hold passionately, and I tend to express them openly. At times I have done so harshly and with judgment. My attitude always, *always* comes back to haunt me when I am aggressive or hostile about my opposition. I still have to work hard to overcome these negative impulses. By taking a deep breath and using this affirmation, I save myself a lot of grief. I heartily recommend repeating these words before hitting the send button on those angry emails and Internet posts!

Remember that every act of aggression or anger toward another human being is an act offensive to God. It stunts your spiritual growth and inhibits your ability to welcome abundance into your life. When you are surrounded by the negative energy of conflict, it is impossible for God to pour good fortune and opportunity on you. Besides, why would he want to reward you for behaving in a way that is contrary to his law of loving your brothers and sisters? A good father will not shower his child with lavish gifts when that child is disobedient and destructive. Therefore when you act out of hostility, you are hurting yourself more than you are hurting your opponent. In subsequent chapters on forgiveness and overcoming obstacles, we will explore techniques to release the more deeply held aggressions that we have toward our fellow humans.

Let me be very clear here that *behaving in a peaceful manner does not mean that you can't express an opinion that is in opposition to someone else's!* God gave us intelligence and reason and a sense of judgment and justice so that we could do just that. All you have to do is take a look at Jesus' life to see that he stood up to the established political, social, and religious figures of his time and called them out on those actions he believed to be unjust or just plain wrong. But the approach that you take is all-important. Expressing your difference of opinion in a calm and respectful manner is an act of peace, often one that takes practice.

THE LEGEND OF CHARTRES CATHEDRAL

There has been a center of worship on the site of Chartres Cathedral for thousands of years, and it has been a Christian structure for at least fifteen hundred of those. The cathedral has endured many fires in its history; during the Dark Ages most buildings were susceptible to fire because of a dangerous combination of wooden infrastructures and the open flames of candles and torches.

One of these fires devastated Chartres Cathedral in the eleventh century. Following the catastrophe, the people of the region came together to discuss the plans to rebuild their church. Remember that this was a special community, a place where an unprecedented school of wisdom and faith had endured since the dawn of Christianity. So when it was proposed that an even grander structure replace the old, the people of Chartres embraced the idea and supported it physically, financially, and emotionally in an unprecedented way. To this day, historians cannot account for how Chartres was built. There are no financial records that would indicate how such a vast temple was paid for. A few noble supporters made public donations, but these were not sufficient to scratch the surface of what it cost to create one of the grandest churches in the world.

There are no accountings because the people of Chartres, understanding as they did these pure teachings of Jesus through the Lord's Prayer, largely contributed to its construction as an act of service, as faith in action. They came together as a community to honor something larger than themselves; they came together to celebrate God and to create a monument to their commitment to create heaven on earth.

And they built their cathedral in the spirit of peace.

During the reconstruction of Chartres, Europe was immersed in the Crusades, with the great families of the continent sending their sons off to fight in holy wars across the world. But the people of the region surrounding Chartres understood that to kill in the name of God was a violation of Christ's teachings: Blessed are the peacemakers for they will be called the Children of God. Instead of sending their sons off to an unjust war, they sent their sons to work on the cathedral. Their legacy would be a testament to God built out of stone and glass, not a pattern of hatred and killing in defiance of God's commandments. And so Chartres was built by conscientious objectors who preferred peace over war. Its construction was an act of faith by those who loved their neighbors and worked with them to create a monument of unequaled and enduring beauty.

It is not a coincidence that as the construction of Chartres came to a close, so did the majority of the bloody Crusades overseas. Every act of peace eliminates an impulse of war. With every stone laid at Chartres, peace in the world moved one step closer to being realized.

In the year 1200, the finishing touch was installed at the center of the nave of this exquisite temple: the labyrinth, with its six-petaled rose representing the Lord's Prayer.

Through the centuries, the people of Chartres would be rewarded for their faith, and their legacy of peace and justice would remain as a blessing to succeeding generations. During the French Revolution, when so many churches were looted and destroyed, Chartres was inexplicably left untouched. Although the violent and destructive revolutionaries got as far as the foot of the cathedral steps, they turned back before entering the church and simply walked away from it. Through two world wars, when bombings had destroyed other Gothic structures across France in places like Reims and Vézelay, Chartres was again spared any damage. Chartres was built with a very specific intention toward peace, with a foundation of faith and service, and it holds that intention to this day within its stones. It is God's place, built by God's children, and protected by God.

YOU ARE GOD'S HANDS ON EARTH

The story of Chartres has many layers of meaning. It reminds us of what we can accomplish as a community working in harmony; it reminds us that there are always positive paths that can be chosen over fighting and disharmony. It is the embodiment of the teachings of Jesus in Luke, chapter 6: when a structure is built on the foundation of his truth and teachings, it cannot be destroyed.

There is another lesson here:

Creating is the natural opposite of destroying;
creative action neutralizes destructive impulses.

The next time you feel overcome by anger or aggression, go build something! *Create:* work with your hands, knit, garden, cook, write a song or a poem, paint, make something with your kids. Perform an action that takes you out of the hostile space and puts you in a place of creativity. Doing so is immediately therapeutic; it shifts your attitude into a much healthier place.

We simply have to start with loving each other, even when that is hard to do. Even when others hold different fundamental beliefs, we must love them—in fact, this is particularly important when others hold different beliefs. Jesus reminds us that it is easy to love those who love us but hard to love those who hate us or curse us, yet this is what we are being charged to do. Within the instruction to *love thy neighbor as thyself* and to *do unto others as you would have them do unto you,* we are reminded how urgent it is to treat our brothers and sisters on earth exactly as we wish to be treated. If we can embrace the understanding that Jesus gave us—that *all* men and women are our neighbors—we can and will make the world a far better, more peaceful place.

We are one human family, with no separation under God. God is our benevolent parent, and he views all his children equally. He wants all his children to thrive, and he wants all his children to care for and about each other. If your biological brothers or sisters were in pain or in danger, wouldn't you want to come to their aid? If a child in your family were ill or in peril, wouldn't you do whatever it takes to help that child?

The fact is that many of your brothers and sisters on earth are suffering; millions of children around the world are in peril.

Along my spiritual journey I have studied the lives and work of female leaders in spirituality over the last two thousand years. I have been moved and changed by the works of many brilliant mystics. Significant among these is the sixteenth-century Spanish saint Teresa of Ávila. Teresa was as prolific as she was inspired, a poet and author of great importance. I use a number of her prayers in my own life, but this one moves me particularly when I contemplate the path of service in the third petal of the Chartres rose.

Reminding us that Jesus was tireless in his efforts to heal and restore his fellow man, Teresa tells us:

> *Christ has no body now, but yours.*
> *No hands, no feet on earth, but yours.*
> *Yours are the eyes through which he looks*
> *with compassion on this world.*

Christ has no body now on earth . . . but yours.

It is now our responsibility to do the work that Jesus left us with our own hands and feet; we are charged to see the world through his eyes and with his same, limitless compassion for each other. Every action we take, we do as God's instrument on earth. We must use that responsibility well and wisely; we must be worthy of his trust in us.

The third petal requires you to take a vow of service and to pledge specifically what action you intend to take to improve the lot of humanity. Abundance, the popular subject that follows in the fourth petal, is tied directly to your generosity on the path of service. If you have been generous in your service commitments and faithful in your surrender to God, you are ready to move into the "reward" segment of this practice.

It is necessary to give in order to receive. And besides, it feels so good!

"Ask and it will be given to you, seek and you will find;
knock and the door will be opened to you.
For everyone who asks receives; he who seeks finds;
and to him who knocks, the door will be opened.
Which of you, if his son asks for bread, will give him a stone?
Or if he asks for a fish, will give him a snake?
If you who are imperfect would give good gifts to your children,
how much more will your Father in heaven give good gifts to
those who ask him?

"So in everything, do to others what you would have them do to you,
for this sums up the Law and the Prophets."

Matthew 7:7–12

VIII

The Fourth Petal—Abundance

*T*he *fourth petal* of the rose corresponds to these words of the
prayer:

Give us today our sufficient bread

God wants you to have what you desire. He wants your greatest
joy and abundance to come to you easily and without suffering. As *your
father, he will always provide exactly what you need—and what you ask
for—when you fulfill your spiritual promises and keep your service commitments.*

Lack is not your natural state; you feel it when you are spiritually
unbalanced.

Abundance is your natural state, and it comes to you effortlessly when you are in harmony with your higher power and fulfilling your promises.

THE CYCLE OF ABUNDANCE

In this segment, you will learn a most powerful technique for attracting abundance. While this approach will not bring about *instant* manifestation, it will create intense and *lasting* manifestation—real and tangible abundance that endures in your life. If good things come to those who wait, then amazing things come to those who wait with faith.

The process of attracting abundance is a cycle of five stages, each of which we will work through individually. They are

Gratitude
Clarity
Commitment
Trust
Gratitude

Gratitude

Notice that our manifestation cycle begins and ends with gratitude. First and foremost, if you are living in harmony with Jesus' commandments on love, care about making the world a better place, and have made authentic service commitments, God will ensure that all your basic needs are provided for. If you are also giving thanks daily for all that you have been given thus far, you are even more likely to attract abundance. As you recite the Lord's Prayer, pause on this line to consider it: *Give us today our sufficient bread.* When you do, always acknowledge what you have been given and be grateful for it. You ask God to give you your daily bread, and he does. If you and your family have all the basic necessities to live comfortably, you indeed have much to be thankful for. Do not take your gifts for granted. An enormous percentage of the population of this planet cannot even imagine the prosperity that you likely have in comparison.

The importance of this step in the manifestation cycle cannot be overemphasized. Your abundance multiplies when you show regular and sincere gratitude for all that you have been given thus far. Commit this divine law to memory and it will serve you well for the rest of your life:

> *The authentic law of manifestation*
> *is activated when you are aligned with your higher mission*
> *to serve God, keep your promises, and make the world a better place;*
> *the law is most powerful when you show gratitude*
> *for all that you have been given on a regular basis.*

I call it "The Law of Thank You." Just say "thank you" and say it often—and mean it. I say it out loud all day long. I sing it in little tunes to my kids when I look at their beautiful, healthy faces, for they are my abundance. I announce it from the balcony of my house when I wake up in the morning and see the beauty that surrounds me and see how God keeps his promise every single day. *God is all good all the time,* and for that I shout, sing, and whisper, "Thank you, God," often. I'm blessed and I know it. And I am eternally and thoroughly grateful to my father in heaven who provides those blessings.

God showers gifts on the appreciative. Why wouldn't he? Think about it for a moment. If you provided for people every day, gave them an assortment of different gifts to ensure they were secure and comfortable, wouldn't you want to know that they were grateful for it? Of course you would. And if the recipients of those gifts showed sincere appreciation for everything they were given on a regular basis, wouldn't that make you want to give them even more? Conversely, if you provided generously for someone who rarely or never acknowledged those gifts, would you be inclined to continue to be so generous? Or would you go out and find another, far more grateful person for whom to become the benefactor?

Exercise: **Your Thank-you Note to God**

- Think about all the blessings that have been bestowed upon you in your life recently. Do not take anything for granted: your health, your loved ones, devoted pets, possessions that matter to you, opportunities that have come your way. Make a thorough list.

- Take that list and write a heartfelt thank-you note to God for everything that has been given to you thus far. It can be as long or as short as you need it to be, just so it fully expresses your gratitude for God's gifts to you.

- Now create a few lines of gratitude that you can incorporate into your daily prayer practice that sums up what you have written in your longer thank-you note. If you cannot think of one, try starting with something simple like this:

  Dear God, I am so grateful for all the blessings you have bestowed upon me and appreciate that you continue to bless me with so much. Thank you.

- If you choose to name specific things that you are grateful for on a particular day, feel free to add them as the spirit moves you.

Clarity

Now that you have acknowledged your gratitude, it is time to work on your clarity. You need to be clear on what you want and why you want it. And you really can have just about anything you want in the world. God makes no judgment about what you want. He isn't evaluating your list of desires and saying, "Hmm, that house is a little too big," or "That car is a little too fast," or "That's a little too much money." God, as your benevolent parent, wants you to have all the things that make you feel secure, fulfilled, and happy.

Let's take a closer look at a few of the lines from the Gospel of Matthew that opened this chapter. Jesus says,

> "Which of you, if his son asks for bread, will give him a stone? Or if he asks for a fish, will give him a snake? If you who are imperfect would give good gifts to your children, how much more will your Father in heaven give good gifts to those who ask him?"

It's all right there. God is more generous with his children than most of us can even imagine. But as you are not alone on this planet, you need to take into consideration the well-being of other humans and Mother Earth when you ask him for things. "Isolationist wanting" can be detrimental to all of us. This is why you need to use responsibility and to clarify your desire. Before praying fervently for something, think it through.

Assuming that you have completed all the previous chapters, that you are clear—or getting clearer—on your relationship to God, have embraced your place in the divine plan, and have made a commitment to be of service to your fellow humans and the planet, you have now earned the right to ask God to expand the abundance in your life.

What is it that you desire in your life that you do not have? Try to focus on the quality of life that this desire represents to you, rather than the specific item. For example, if you want to be able to buy a house for your family, do not say, "I want to buy that house at 1234 Maple Drive." Instead say, "I want to buy a house that will be perfect for my family, where we will be safe and happy, and that will have all the following qualities . . ."

If you are looking for lasting love, do not say, "I want John [or Jane] to love me." Instead say, "I want to find the right mate with whom I can have a loving and committed relationship, one who has the following qualities . . ."

The reason I caution you against being too specific is this: sometimes what you think you want is not what is best for you, and only God knows that because only God sees the entire divine plan unfolding. So while you may think that the house at 1234 Maple Drive is perfect for you, God may know of a house that is far better! Maple Drive may have termites, or perhaps the school district it is in is not the best for your child, or any number of other things that you cannot even imagine but that God already knows. We will explore this concept in greater detail at the "trust" stage of this process.

Exercise: **What You Desire and Why You Desire It**

- Write down one thing that you want to manifest in your life, for yourself. It can be anything: a house for your family, true love, a child, improved health, a job opportunity, more money to pay off your debts, a dependable car. The sky's the limit, so choose whatever you want. And choose something for yourself this time! You will be praying every day for other people, so now you get to focus on your own needs. For this exercise, just choose one thing to focus on.

- Write down why you want this particular thing. How will it make you feel? What will it do to improve the quality of your life? What are all the reasons you can think of for wanting this? If you can't come up with good answers to these questions, maybe you should reconsider your request! You should feel passionate about your request; it should be something that you want with all your heart. This kind of passion is your spirit's method of alerting you to what you need. Remember in a previous chapter when you learned that your dreams are not an accident? That they are signposts for what you should be doing with your life? So are your greatest desires signposts for that which will make you feel truly fulfilled.

- Read your request and your reasons out loud to God. Always finish by saying, "If this is in harmony with your will and the divine plan."

Commitment

God knows that the more secure and fulfilled you are, the more likely you will be to share your good fortune with the world around you. This is human nature. So God now has two motives for bestowing your greatest desires upon you. The first is his natural parental love that makes him want to see his children happy. The second is his knowledge that the most obedient and grateful children will share their abundance and fulfill their service commitments when they are given their heart's desires. Which brings us to commitment, the next level of the manifestation cycle.

Exercise: **Reaffirming Your Commitment**

- Go back to the desire you wrote about in the last exercise. Write down how receiving this specific desire will help you fulfill your commitment toward improving the state of the world. For example, if you are seeking a partner whom you can spend your life with, perhaps you are looking for someone who shares your interests and who can work with you in your commitment to make the world better. For example, "I want to meet someone who cares about animals as much as I do so that we can rescue them together." Or if you desire a new car, perhaps it is so you can have a dependable vehicle that will allow you to deliver meals to the infirm. Perhaps a new car will free up more of the time that you would normally spend waiting for public transportation; that time can then be used in other, service-oriented ways.

- If you cannot think of how your desire could impact the world in any measurable way, then attach a service pledge to your desire. For example, "If you grant me this, I will donate time or money to XYZ charity."

Let me give you an example of how a desire that appears "unspiritual" on the surface can actually be of great benefit to the planet. I have a friend who really wanted to buy an exotic European sports car, but he felt a little guilty about it because he is not typically a flashy consumer. We'll call him James. Now, James happens to have a real passion for cars, a passion he and his brothers inherited from their father. James grew up going to car shows with his dad and his brothers, so for him, such a car would represent his happy childhood and bring him a kind of fulfillment he could not get from anything else. He also knew that owning such a car would make his father and brothers excited for him and proud of him. He would be a success in their eyes, and this was a major motivation for James. He cared deeply about what his family thought and how they viewed him.

Earlier in this chapter we learned that God doesn't pass judgment on what you want and why you want it, as long as it is harmonious with the divine plan. This is also why none of us should pass judgment on what others desire, as we don't know the deeper emotional reasons or attachments that are at the root of these wishes. In James's case, the car, symbolic of approval from his family, was an emblem of success for him. And yet because James realized that this wasn't the most spiritual of requests, he pledged to donate to charity when he bought the car. Guess what? A very rare model came available, and at an extraordinarily low price because the owner was leaving the country and wanted to sell it quickly. James bought his dream car, and every time he makes a car payment, he also makes a monthly contribution to the cause that he pledged to support.

But the story doesn't end there. James has also discovered that many people see his car as a symbol of success. They want to know how he got the car. And so James uses every opportunity to reinforce his service-based prayer process by sharing it with those who will listen. What on the surface appeared to be an "unspiritual" desire to buy a sports car has given James the opportunity to fulfill his service commitments on a number of levels, while receiving exactly what he wanted!

Trust

The story of James and his car brings us to the next step in the process of attracting abundance, which is *trust*. You have to trust God and surrender to the divine plan. While your father in heaven wants to give you everything you want, he also wants to be sure that all those things are in your best interest. For example, my friend James happens to be a really level-headed, responsible guy. If instead he had a reckless nature, perhaps God would not have made it so easy for him to manifest his superfast car! James has work to do here on earth, and God does not want to see him in a high-speed accident. So if James had not been able to manifest his desire, he would have needed to trust that there was a good reason that he did not receive it. God, in such a case, would actually be protecting him rather than punishing him.

In chapter 6 of the Gospel of Matthew, where Jesus tells us how to pray, he also tells us that God already knows what we want and what we need before we ask him. This is an important reminder, not just of God's omniscience but of the fact that *God is far more creative than we are. He has more resources than we can possibly imagine, and what he has in store for us is much bigger than anything we can think of ourselves.* This is why I emphasize that you should not be too specific in the details of your requests and that you must trust divine process. You can be very clear on the *quality of life* or the *nature of the desire*, but it is often best not to request specific items or circumstances.

> *One of the biggest mistakes you can make*
> *when praying for abundance*
> *is limiting yourself by being too specific.*

I must pause here for a moment to address those of you who have read the recent rash of "law of attraction" books. Most of you are likely now completely confused because those programs tell you to do exactly the opposite of what I am suggesting. They tell you to ask for what you want and to be very specific. They emphasize that you should have a really sound understanding of exactly what you desire, in detail, so that you are being very clear to "the universe" about what gifts it should bestow upon you.

Bad idea.

Why? Because:

*Being specific when asking God for something
suggests that you know more than He does.*

It's spiritual arrogance. And it's simply not in your best interest. Trust God's unlimited nature. You just may get the most astonishing surprise of your life!

THE PARABLE OF THE LABORER
AND THE BOOTS

Long ago there lived a man called Frederick who worked hard to provide for his wife and his children by taking odd jobs as a laborer in his village. Frederick and his family lived from day to day on the meager wages he could earn in his little community. They sustained themselves in this way until the day that a plague swept through the village. While Frederick's family was spared from the plague, they no longer had any means of income, as the illness had wiped out the majority of their community.

Frederick knew that he would have to leave his village to find work. The nearest town was a long walk, several miles away, but there was no other option. He began the journey on the rough and rocky road toward town, but the thin soles of his worn-out shoes could not protect his feet from the sharp rocks of the road. By the time he arrived in the town, they were cut and bleeding.

Frederick was able to find work, but his feet hurt so much that he wasn't sure how he was going to endure the walk back and forth into town each day. He simply could not afford to buy new shoes. That afternoon as he prepared for the excruciating walk home, he stopped to gaze into the window of the cobbler's shop. There he saw a pair of beautiful boots with thick, solid soles.

"Now, those are exactly what I need!" Frederick thought. "If I had boots that sturdy, I could walk for miles each day with no pain!"

The price of the boots was a fortune, the equivalent of a month's worth of food for his family. Yet he became fixated on his need for the boots. Frederick was sure they were the solution to his problem.

One day, on his slow and painful walk into the town, Frederick decided to take a detour to walk along the riverbank. While this route into town was longer, the ground near the water's edge was softer and gentler on his ravaged feet. As he walked, he heard a sharp cry around the bend ahead. The cry grew louder: it was a man shouting urgently for help. Frederick ran as fast as his damaged feet would take him until he found the source of the distress.

A richly dressed man was waving a walking stick frantically toward the river. "My son! My boy has fallen into the river and he cannot swim! Nor can I! Please help us!"

Frederick, who had grown up swimming in this river, did not hesitate. He jumped in where he saw the frantic splash, and a few seconds later had his hands on the boy, bringing him to the surface for air. Frederick swam to the shore and delivered the boy—worse for wear, but alive—to the feet of his father.

Later that evening as Frederick dined at the town inn at the request of the elegant man and his recovered son, he learned that his host was the lord of the neighboring lands and the boy was his only son and heir. They had stopped to water their horses, and the child had lost his footing and fallen into the river.

"I cannot think of how to repay you, my friend," said the elegant lord. "You have saved my son and my family, which is a gift beyond measure. Tell me, what can I give you as a reward?"

Frederick could not believe his ears as he looked down at the shreds that represented shoes on his feet. He could see those beautiful boots from the cobbler's window—boots that were made to grace the feet of a lord such as this—in his mind's eye. Hadn't he been dreaming about them these past days? He said to the man, "Sir, there is a pair of boots that I have had my eye on . . ."

The lord attempted to interrupt, but Frederick, in his excitement and his certainty, could hear nothing else. He had been focused on this solution and now it had come to pass. God was indeed generous and merciful.

"I must have those boots, my lord! They will protect my feet and enable my work! They are the only thing I truly desire!"

Frederick was so enthusiastic about the boots, so insistent, that the lord dispatched a runner to bring the cobbler to Frederick. The shoemaker arrived with the boots and tailored them to Frederick's feet. The boots were, indeed, the strongest and most comfortable footwear imaginable, and Frederick all but danced home to show them to his wife.

As Frederick left the inn, the wealthy lord watched him go, shaking his head. "Strange," said the man to his son. "I would have given him anything—a carriage and horses, a bag of gold—absolutely anything he wanted, and more. And yet he was so fixated on receiving those boots that he wouldn't allow me to suggest all these other gifts that I wished to bestow upon him!"

And so Frederick, content to have his boots, walked miles to the town each day to work as a laborer. He was happy enough, having received his specific wish—and never knowing that he could have had so much more than he ever imagined.

I have told the parable of Frederick's boots to some who have groaned and replied, "But that's so obvious. Who would really settle for a pair of boots when they could have anything?" The answer is almost everyone, because we have forgotten that we really can have anything.

Here is an example. A friend of mine was diligently using one of the "law of attraction" practices that had recently become popular. The process instructed that he concentrate on what he wanted very specifically, which he did. He was having difficulty making ends meet financially and therefore focused on landing a promotion, which would give him a significant raise. After a few weeks of dedicated effort, he was chosen for the promotion, and with it, he received the raise that he wanted.

So that's a happy ending, right? Well, no, it isn't, because he hated his job and the company was run by an abusive tyrant. Landing the promotion just added to his stress and made him more miserable. The raise he received was small compensation for the number of hours and the new responsibility he had added to his workload. Most of all, the promotion took him farther away from his real dreams, as he no longer had time to pursue anything other than work.

Frederick received the boots he wished for, but he still had to walk miles to work each day. My friend received the promotion he envisioned, but he still worked in a job that made him unhappy and dreaded Mondays like nobody's business. Both men in these circumstances could have surrendered their problems to God and allowed the unlimited wisdom and generosity of divine intelligence to enter their lives and truly solve their problems. Had my friend given the same amount of energy toward strengthening his connection to God and reconnecting with his destiny through prayer and introspection, his outcome would assuredly have been more satisfying in the long run.

God is better at this than any of us can fathom. Allow him to work in your life in his unlimited way.

EMBRACE YOUR MOST BENEVOLENT INVESTOR AND PARTNER

Over the last few years, after the extraordinary way in which God answered my prayers, I decided to get serious about sharing this process with the people around me. Like the friend in the aforementioned story, I saw many people I cared about living in a self-made and unfulfilled world of frustration. I knew that this prayer process would transform their lives as it had mine if I could just get them to realign their thinking. Many of my friends are artists or of an entrepreneurial spirit, people who are trying to create their own businesses and become their own bosses. For most of them, their prayer requests involve having the money and security to leave their "day job" so that they can pursue their true bliss. I created this exercise for them, and it has proven to be both popular and effective.

Exercise: **What If Bill or Oprah Were Your Business Partner?**
In this exercise, you will imagine that either Bill Gates or Oprah Winfrey is your good friend and your business partner. You pick. I chose those two icons not only because they are wealthy and powerful but because they are philanthropic.

As your business partner and good friend, Bill or Oprah would certainly want you to be successful and happy. But they both possess brilliant and savvy business minds, so they are not going to invest in just anything. Your job is to convince them that your new business idea or project should be fully funded and given whatever support you need to get it off the ground, as soon as possible.

- Write the summary of a business plan that you would give to Bill or Oprah. Describe your business/your art/your idea, and give as many details about the essence and quality of the project as you think are necessary to show why you are unique and worthy of support and investment.

- The plan should include what you need to get started and sustain the business. What resources are necessary for your success? List everything you need, but do not limit yourself in terms of amounts and quantities.

- Remembering that both Bill and Oprah are humanitarians, show them that you are as well by aligning your new business with a charitable cause. How are you going to do this? What is your short-term and long-term plan for philanthropy as your business flourishes?

- How will the success of your business/project change your life? Your family? The world?

If you answered all the questions thoroughly, you should now have a pretty good idea of what your ideal circumstance would look like for your new business or project. And in light of that, I have some good news and some bad news.

Bad news: Bill Gates is not your business partner. Neither is Oprah Winfrey. They will not be investing in you anytime in the foreseeable future.

Good news: God is your business partner. He will be investing in you. Isn't God bigger than Bill Gates and Oprah Winfrey? He has even more unlimited assets and is more able to provide for you than any human on earth. And you have access to him twenty-four hours a day, seven days a week, without going through assistants and publicists. You can achieve everything in this business plan and more because your partner is omnipotent!

Use this affirmation whenever necessary as you continue to pray for financial and occupational freedom:

God is my business partner. Everything I need and desire to live my bliss is available to me through God's investment and support.

BELIEVE FIRST,
THEN YOU CAN ASK AND RECEIVE

Let us take a final look at the verse in the New Testament that is most often quoted in "law of attraction" programs, like the one that tells you all you have to do is *ask, believe, receive.*

This is Matthew, chapter 21, verses 21 and 22 (emphasis mine):

> "I tell you the truth: if you have faith and do not doubt . . . you can say to this mountain, 'Go, throw yourself into the sea,' and it will be done. *If you believe*, you will *receive* whatever you *ask* for in prayer."

Most "law of attraction" practices take these words out of order, putting *ask* before *believe*. This is the fundamental flaw in their formula. The key word here is *believe*—how it is defined and where it is placed in the equation. The proponents of instant manifestation would likely tell you that it means you simply have to believe that you can attract whatever it is you desire at any time. But this is unfortunately a shallow interpretation of a very deep lesson because the verse is taken out of its original context. When we consider the deep spiritual context of the surrounding chapters in the Gospel of Matthew (21:12 to 22:45), we begin to understand that when Jesus instructs us to believe, he is referring to the all-powerful and benevolent nature of God and to our own effortless access to that essence. We are to *believe* that God can do anything, first and foremost. By strengthening our connection to God through that belief—which is defined here as faith—combined with surrender and service, we may then *ask* for what we require and *receive* it with joy and gratitude.

This is a powerful teaching that Jesus has bestowed upon us. When extracted from that context and used for the sole sake of material manifestation, it is misleading and diminished. It is time to restore the grace and depth of these words to their proper place within our spiritual instruction, a lesson about the sincere light of faith that can transform lives and change the world.

Gratitude

We are reminded finally that our manifestation cycle is a circle that begins and ends with gratitude. You must continue to acknowledge what you have been given and be grateful for it. You have asked God to give you your sufficient bread, and he has delivered what you desire and require. You have more and more to be thankful for each day, and you are now enlightened enough to never take your gifts for granted.

And here is the added beautiful bonus that comes with celebrating in the fourth petal. In the ancient mystery school teacings, the word for wisdom rhymed with the word for bread—*lochma* and *hochma*. There is an esoteric pun here, wordplay that reminds us that our true abundance comes from the appreciation of sacred knowledge. Our sufficient bread does not come to us solely in the manner of material security but also through the greater understanding of God's unlimited nature and our blessed place within his divine plan.

The path of the fourth petal, abundance, teaches that you *can* have it all, and you can make a difference in the world while you acquire everything you need and desire. If that isn't miraculous, I don't know what is! And now that you're feeling so blessed by God's generosity, you should also be feeling very benevolent. This is the perfect time to dig a little deeper and explore the healing path of forgiveness.

"For if you forgive men when they sin against you,
your heavenly Father will also forgive you.
But if you do not forgive men their sins,
your Father will not forgive your sins."

Matthew 6:14–15

IX

The Fifth Petal—Forgiveness

Forgiveness

*T*he fifth petal of the rose corresponds to these words of the prayer:

> *Forgive us our debts,*
> *as we also have forgiven our debtors.*

The inability, or reluctance, to forgive is our greatest failing. It is the cause of the majority of personal strife as well as global war. When you hold on to your anger, resentment, or disappointment in other people, you sabotage your own happiness. You use your precious spiritual energy on those negative emotions, when you could be using that power to live a joyous life, attract abundance, and improve the conditions of the world around you. An inability or unwillingness to forgive constricts you, draws you inward, whereas forgiveness gives you the opportunity to expand and open the channels of abundance in your life.

Forgiveness is the great eraser of destructive emotions. But forgiving can be a very difficult thing to do, because most of us are out of practice. We aren't generally taught to forgive. If we were, the world would look very different than it does today. I assure you that forgiveness gets easier with repetition, but you need to apply concentrated effort on a regular basis to really get the hang of it.

I want to set the tone for this most sacred element of the Lord's Prayer with a true story about the human spirit that has inspired me for over thirteen years. It is the most extraordinary tale of forgiveness that I have ever encountered. If you are holding on to hostility, anger, or even hatred toward another human being, I hope that you will feel differently when you finish this story.

FINDING FORGIVENESS:
THE EXTRAORDINARY LEGACY OF
AMY BIEHL AND HER FAMILY

Amy Biehl was a brilliant, compassionate, socially conscious student at Stanford University, and a Fulbright scholar. In 1992 she relocated to Cape Town, South Africa, to work in the communities that had been decimated by apartheid, the institutionalized racism that had plagued South Africa and resulted in reprehensible discrimination and subsequent violence since 1948. Amy worked with the underprivileged in the black townships, and in preparation for the first "free elections" that would allow blacks to vote, she labored to promote voter registration there. Everyone who worked with Amy spoke of her passion to improve the conditions in South Africa and her dedication to promote tolerance, equality, and education across racial lines.

On August 25, 1993, after a day of working to register black voters, Amy drove through the township of Gugulethu outside Cape Town. She was in the wrong place at the wrong time. An angry demonstration over racial discrimination was just breaking up, and a gang of young men, spotting Amy in her car, decided to make an example of her. The men were black, Amy was white. This was the only factor they took into account in a terrible instant of rage. The men had no way of knowing that Amy was an ally, a crusader for change and equality. At that moment, she was a symbol to them of what had oppressed their people in South Africa for so long, an emblem of a horrific racial divide. The men stoned Amy's car to force her to stop, then dragged her out of the car and into the mob.

What happened next is almost too nightmarish to repeat. Amy was murdered at the hands of the mob: stoned, beaten with bricks, and then ultimately stabbed to death. The promising light of Amy Biehl was extinguished at the age of twenty-six.

Four of Amy's killers were tried for murder and subsequently sentenced to eighteen years in prison. But amnesty opportunities came to them through South Africa's Truth and Reconciliation Commission, an investigative body formed by Nelson Mandela to investigate crimes that occurred during the heated tensions of apartheid.

Amy's parents, Linda and Peter Biehl, attended the amnesty hearing for Amy's killers in 1998. While in attendance they did something completely unexpected: the Biehls expressed their forgiveness and asked the judge to pardon the men who had murdered their daughter. They pleaded for their amnesty with grace and eloquence, emphasizing the need for dialogue to replace violence. And when that amnesty was granted, the Biehls shook hands with the young men who had taken the life of their child.

The men responsible for Amy's death were released after serving four years in prison.

For many of us, the actions of Amy Biehl's parents are perhaps unimaginable. But for Linda and Peter Biehl, forgiveness was the only way that they felt could properly honor their daughter's memory. As the Biehls said in a public statement at the time, "Amy was drawn to South Africa and she admired the vision of Nelson Mandela. . . . It is this vision of forgiveness and reconciliation that we have honored."

Rather than running away from the nightmare that South Africa must have represented for them, they created the Amy Biehl Foundation to continue their daughter's work. In the same township where Amy was killed, the foundation established youth programs, discussion groups, and community projects to create jobs. The parents worked with all their hearts and minds to promote peace and heal the pain of half a century of violence caused by racial discrimination. The essence of forgiveness spread, first restoring the spirits of the Biehl family, then aiding in the rehabilitation of the men who killed Amy while also bringing comfort to the parents and families of those men, all of whom had been victims in their own way. The families were healed, the community restored, and the energy of forgiving and loving thy neighbor radiates as an inspiration to the rest of us.

I have used the lesson of Linda and Peter Biehl as my touchstone for forgiveness many times over the last thirteen years. When I am having a particularly hard time getting past some kind of slight, attack, or "trespass against me," I always think back to what the Biehl family was able to do. It reminds me that anything I have endured is minuscule compared to what they overcame in their lives, and I find strength in holding myself up to their standard of grace.

I realize, in light of the Biehl family's example, that being unforgiving diminishes me, and I have pledged to learn from them. Amy's legacy continues.

Exercise: **How Much Forgiveness Is in You?**
I find that when I tell the Biehls' story, the majority of the people respond in the same way that I did—with tears and with awe. They are inspired to test this complete and unconditional approach to forgiveness in their own lives.

But not everyone reacts this way. Some people simply cannot comprehend this level of forgiveness. They cannot imagine finding forgiveness in the face of such terrible violence and tragedy. If you are also having trouble imagining that you could find this level of forgiveness in yourself, let me emphasize something of critical importance:

> *By learning from these extreme examples,*
> *you will never have to repeat them.*

The legacy of Amy Biehl is a gift to all of us, as it gives us the opportunity to learn an important spiritual lesson, perhaps the most important lesson, through a dramatic example. We can gain the benefit of real healing and wisdom through understanding and embracing these lessons of forgiveness without having to endure any of the tragedy ourselves. Talk about something to be grateful for!

- Think about the Amy Biehl story and the actions of her parents, who forgave their daughter's killers and even worked alongside them to rebuild their community. Do you believe you would be capable of forgiveness in such extreme circumstances?

- Now make a list of everyone you are currently holding a grudge against. Go back as far as you have to. Write down why you are holding on to anger, resentment, or hurt in relation to these individuals. Now ask yourself if you can forgive them their human failings. Compare the "debts" or "trespasses" of the people on your list to the "debts" that the men who killed Amy Biehl owed to her family. Does this help you reach in deeper to find forgiveness?

PEOPLE ARE DOING THE BEST THEY CAN WITH WHAT THEY HAVE

People will disappoint you in life, and they will disappoint you often. Yet each person who hurts you or causes you some sort of disillusionment is actually doing you a favor. They are providing you with opportunities to prove how unconditionally you can love and forgive your brothers and sisters under God. It is easy to love those who love you, but as Jesus reminds us in Luke 6:28, it is very difficult to "bless those who curse you." Jesus asks a lot of us with this statement, but you can benefit immensely if you can put it into practice.

All people are damaged. When they behave badly, it is often because of pain that has accumulated from their past. Sometimes, when someone we know well hurts us, we are able to see clearly what may have caused their behavior. But when dealing with strangers, business associates, or people we just don't know that well, we have very little information about their personal history. We don't know what has happened in those people's lives to cause them pain. We don't know about their childhood, and we don't know what may have happened to them earlier in the day or just before you walked through their door! It is for this reason that I use the following affirmation:

People are doing the best they can with what they have.

This is almost always true. Whether it's a snarky customer service rep on the telephone, your boss, or your spouse, people are trying to get by day to day with the coping skills that they possess. Show compassion, and repeat that affirmation when you begin to feel irritated. How many times have you hung up the phone or walked away from somebody's office shaking your head and thinking, "Gosh, what got into *him* today?" Even the nicest people in the world have bad moments. Perhaps you just encountered someone at a bad time. It happens every day. I know that I would not want my character to be judged for a transgression I made when I was under pressure, exhausted, or upset about something.

I once had a complete meltdown in a bank, screaming so loud at the teller that security was called to escort me out of the building. Now, let me state for the record that I do not normally behave this way. However, this was the same day that the pediatric endocrinologist had told me that my little Shane would not live to see his second birthday. My nerves were shot. The bank teller, who probably still tells the story of the crazy screaming lady, had no idea what kind of emotional devastation I had lived through and had no way of knowing that I was reacting to other, potentially tragic circumstances in my life.

We all have these dark human moments, and we all have to cut each other some slack as a result, because people are doing the best they can with what they have. And you have no idea what that perfect stranger is going through in his or her own life today.

If you really want to make spiritual progress, you can and should pray for the healing and happiness of those who may have "trespassed against you." When you pray for those who have hurt you the most, those who have really wronged you, your prayer benefits the world and aids in your own spiritual growth. Dramatically. It makes God happy, and it increases your ability to attract goodness and abundance into your life. Carrying a grudge multiplies the energy of darkness and constricts your own opportunities for happiness, as forgiving increases the light and expands your own possibilities for joy.

NO ONE CAN STEAL YOUR DESTINY

Sometimes when someone hurts us, we bemoan the circumstance and ask, "Why? Why did this happen when I can see no possible good coming from it and I did the right thing?" I bet you can think of any number of circumstances that left you scratching your head and asking, "What was that all about?"

Here is the answer, another universal law:

It isn't all about you all the time.

Does that sound harsh? It really isn't. It's actually very liberating. *Sometimes people come into our lives because it is our duty to give them opportunity: the opportunity to fulfill their own promise, the chance to do the right thing.* But one of God's gifts to us is free will, so each of us has the ability to choose to do the right thing—or not. So while we are fulfilling our part of the promise by working with people openly and with trust, if they betray that trust or behave in a negative or destructive way, it is their choice to do so. When that happens, we are challenged to pray for them, forgive them, and move on. We have fulfilled our spiritual obligation as long as we have acted with integrity through the process.

This approach can apply to both business and personal relationships, and sometimes both at the same time. Here is an example from my own life that really helped me to understand this concept and not get subsequently trapped in a morass of bitterness.

After finishing a draft of my novel about Mary Magdalene, *The Expected One,* I went in search of an agent to represent me and the book, which was the result of fifteen years of work. Looking for representation—and validation—while facing rejection is a tough process that most of us in the arts have to go through, and it can be very disheartening. So of course I was thrilled when contacted by a very successful and talented literary agent who expressed interest in my book. After reading my manuscript, she wanted to meet with me; we were both excited about the possibility of working together. I sat with her for hours in her office as she paged through my manuscript, asked questions, and gave me ideas to perhaps make the book more marketable. I worked with this woman for the better part of a year. She told me repeatedly that she would sign me as a client officially and get busy showing my book to publishers just as soon as she was sure that the manuscript was where it needed to be. I had no reason to believe otherwise, and I continued to wait. In the meantime, I also rejected other offers, because I was committed to working with her, and I believed that she felt the same.

And then, quite suddenly, she sent me a single-sentence email that said, "After much consideration, I have decided that I cannot represent you."

That was it. No explanation, no apology, no acknowledgment that we had been working together for a year. She simply and unceremoniously dumped me.

Of course, I was devastated. And angry. Not just at her but at God. How could he have paired me up with someone who would waste a year of my time? Not only did I now have to start over in the very difficult search for an agent, but my book had been kept off the market for a full year. I believed in that book with all my heart and soul. I knew that the information in it would make a difference in a lot of people's lives, just as it had in mine. I had to believe that God wanted me to publish a book with a message about love, faith, and forgiveness. So why did he waste a year of my time?

And the answer is: he didn't. None of that time was wasted, because all of it figured into a divine plan of which I am only one single element and which I cannot even begin to understand completely. I learned a lot from that experience, and the first lesson was this: *it wasn't about me.* It was partially about giving that agent the chance to be a part of the work I was creating, because perhaps God wanted her to have that opportunity. On some level, we were supposed to work together for *her* learning and benefit, as much as mine. She chose by her free will not to participate in my work, and whatever her reasons were, they are honestly none of my business in the long run.

But I did gain another enormous spiritual perk from this experience, as it came with the lesson:

No one can steal your destiny.

No matter what anyone "does to you" along your path to either personal or professional happiness, that person cannot interfere with your destiny. Only you are in control of that, within the master plan created with God. You will encounter setbacks in this crazy world of seven billion souls that will frustrate and challenge you. We all do. But *your destiny cannot be changed or diminished by another human being's actions when you are firmly on your path toward carrying out God's plans.*

The old adage "When one door closes, another one opens" is absolutely true. God will always provide new opportunities for you if the actions of another interfere with your divine mission. Such interference is only temporary. How can it be anything else? God is bigger than any human being's free will, and he will always steer you in another, healthier, and more abundant direction. The divine architect will not have his master plan thwarted because one of the laborers doesn't want to do his or her part on the building site that day. He will find new laborers for you to partner with so that you can continue to build your own monument. And when you know that all such setbacks are temporary, you will find it much easier to forgive humans for being human.

People are doing the best they can with what they have.

You can probably guess that my story doesn't end there. Rather than dwelling on my anger, I prayed for that agent, and I prayed most of all that she would never dismiss an aspiring writer with quite so much disdain ever again. I prayed that she would recognize her treatment of me so that she would not hurt anyone else in the same way. Perhaps that was the real point of the experience. And then I let it go and moved on, knowing that God would open other doors for me. Which he did. Lots of them. And they were bigger and better opportunities than any that I could have had within the old circumstances. I could write a separate inspirational book just about the new agent who came into my life and how he changed it miraculously through his unconditional support of me and my work. He was the angel who helped me find my destiny and fulfill my dreams. Which leads us to the final lesson of this concept:

> *The more forgiving you are,*
> *the faster the new opportunities will come your way.*

Have you ever been in a car with a GPS system? If you have, then you know that you type in your destination and an electronic map appears, usually accompanied by a voice that tells you how to get to your desired location. But if you make a wrong turn and cannot follow the original directions laid out for you, the GPS system recalculates automatically. It takes into consideration the altered direction you are now heading in and then creates a new path to get to your desired destination. It is the perfect metaphor for what God does when you are forced to change course. He recalculates and sends you to your original destination, but by a different route.

The more you experience these setbacks, the better you get at learning not only to acknowledge them as part of God's plan but to actually appreciate them. Peter and I now refer to this concept as "God's GPS system," and when someone lets us down, we wait with anticipation to see how God is going to readjust our course. It can be a lot of fun to see what amazing journey he will send you on!

Exercise: **For Whom Can You Pray Today?**

- Choose one person from your recent past who has caused you pain or who somehow has had an impact on your "destiny." It can be someone who took "your" promotion or the person you were dating who just suddenly stopped calling. The more intense the circumstance, the better. The harder it is for you to find forgiveness for this person, the more powerful your own healing will be.

- Pray that this individual may find healing, that he or she may find light where there has been darkness. Pray that he or she may find relief for whatever pain haunts him or her in his or her own life, and that he or she may not hurt anyone in the future the way that he or she has hurt you. Your prayer could save someone else heartache in the future, and that is a divine and generous act. Even if you cannot ultimately affect the free will of another, you are putting energy toward that person's healing and enlightenment and will therefore have made the world a better place within that single prayer.

- If the person is someone who has no further place in your life, let him or her go. Use this affirmation as needed:

I forgive and release (person's name) from my life with love, and I pray that he/she finds healing on his/her own path and harms no one.

Just to be clear, forgiving someone doesn't mean you have to keep that individual in your life. Some people are simply going to have a toxic effect on you if you allow them to stay, and you will have to move away from them. It is *how* you end those relationships that will affect your spiritual progress. If you can love them, forgive them, and release them in a way that wishes them only healing, you will make excellent progress. If you cannot, you need to spend some more time focused on this fifth petal of the rose as you say the Lord's Prayer every day. Lack of forgiveness will hold you back and cause you to become spiritually stagnant. You may want to add this:

Dear God, please help me find the strength and love within myself to forgive others so that I may move forward on my path in your service.

FORGIVENESS BEGINS WITH YOURSELF

And here is another benefit of praying for someone who has hurt you: each time you forgive someone and pray for him or her, that energy of forgiveness surrounds you. This allows someone in your life who may carry anger or resentment toward you to find forgiveness more easily in your direction. Which brings us to the part of the prayer that says

Forgive us our debts

Forgiveness begins within yourself, which is why the prayer contains this line. It is important that you turn your ability to forgive inward and rid yourself of the shame-based emotions that build up and create the spiritual equivalent of toxic waste. If you somehow believe that you "deserve" to have bad things happen to you or that you are the victim of your own "bad karma," then you need to get rid of that belief quickly. In order to do so effectively, you must take stock of those whom you may have offended along the way.

Exercise: **To Whom Do You Owe a Debt?**

- Make a list of people whom you feel you may have let down or disappointed. Who out there is possibly praying for *you* because of your actions? Include everyone you can think of who may have been hurt by your actions, intentionally or unintentionally.
- What have you learned from any of these circumstances about yourself and your own behavior? How could you have reacted differently, and how will you behave differently in the future as a result?
- Express your sincere desire to heal the pain of those relationships in your prayers. Acknowledge to God that you are aware that you caused pain to others with your actions, that you are fully accountable, and that you have learned and will move on.
- Forgive yourself. You are learning and growing, and each of these instances is a lesson on your path.

Remember always this great commandment that Jesus left for us in Matthew 7:1–2:

"Do not judge, or you too will be judged. For in the same way you judge others, you will be judged."

Don't judge the actions of others, as you do not know the secrets of their heart or destiny. Be compassionate with your fellow humans, and be gentle with yourself. And when others around you fall, help them to get up again. The next time you find yourself on the ground, you may be surprised at whose hand is there to help you up.

> *Forgiveness is the great equalizer.*
> *It costs you nothing but buys you everything.*

Now that you have made such extraordinary spiritual progress through the path of the Lord's Prayer, you are ready to take on the big issues awaiting you in the sixth petal: sin and evil. These are the final blocks to your spiritual progress and ultimate happiness, so they must be eliminated!

Don't worry. They're not nearly as bad as they sound, because both of them are entirely in your control.

"There is no sin.
It is you who make sin exist when you act
according to the habits of your corrupted nature;
This is where sin lies."

The Gospel of Mary Magdalene

X

The Sixth Petal—Overcoming Obstacles

Overcoming

And do not bring us into temptation,
but deliver us from evil.

To reap the power of these final words of the Lord's Prayer, we must agree on the definition of three terms: *temptation*, *sin*, and *evil*. We'll start with evil, for two reasons. First, because the power of evil can feel overwhelming and you must understand that it is not; second, because defining evil clears the way to understanding temptation and sin.

What is evil? It's a question that theologians and philosophers have debated for thousands of years. I will not embark upon a lengthy analysis of all those possibilities here. Instead I will state a definition that was given to me while studying the medieval prayer process from Chartres. It is a very simple yet powerful definition:

> *That which keeps you*
> *from accomplishing your mission*
> *and fulfilling your divine promise*
> *is defined as evil.*

Evil is not an exterior force or a horned devil that will tempt you off your path. It is the failing of your own nature. Within the larger framework of evil lies temptation. *Temptation* is the human weakness that can lead us into *sin*.

So what, then, is sin? Try this on:

> *Sin is a self-imposed limitation*
> *that causes us to stray*
> *from our path of service and from our remembering*
> *that we are one with God through love and forgiveness.*

Therefore, *temptation to sin* causes us to forget our spiritual lessons and leads to *evil*, which keeps us from fulfilling our destiny and keeping our sacred promises to God.

CONQUERING THE SEVEN DEADLY SINS

Most often, this spiral toward evil begins with one of the intoxicating yet corrosive *seven deadly sins*. It is significant to note that when this list of "sins" first appeared in the Christian writings of the fourth century, they were referred to as the *patterns of evil thought*. This is a succinct and accurate definition of how these obstacles were meant to be viewed. The list was originally created as a constructive tool, to help the faithful identify their spiritual weaknesses so that they would have guidelines to follow on the path to leading a purer life with God. It was two hundred years later, after many of the early Christians were declared heretics (often for the more independent and less institutionalized nature of their beliefs) that this tool became a more structured list that pointed to an imperiled soul. Pope Gregory the Great first organized the list into the form most recognized today, the seven deadly sins.

These patterns of evil thought, call them what you will, matter immensely as they are the evils that you must be delivered from in order to stay in harmony with your highest and most divine nature. They are the temptations you must resist if you are to attract everything that you desire into your life and keep it there. They are the manner in which humans inflict suffering upon themselves. It is through understanding what they are and how to conquer them that we are released from spiritual bondage.

These are sins against ourselves and our fellow man; they are emotions that cause us to behave in ways that do not serve our higher purpose and that keep us from enlightenment. Most of all, *they are patterns of thought that stand in opposition to love.* They are

Ego
Anger
Envy
Complacency
Greed
Indulgence
Lust

We will look at each individually, because we all have a dangerous weakness toward at least one!

EGO
(SOMETIMES LISTED AS PRIDE OR HUBRIS)

Ego is contained within all the other sins; it is frequently at the root of them, which is why it's first on the list.

If you think of ego as a "pattern of evil thought," it is valuing one's self over God, over God's plan, and over God's other children. It is investing in the belief that everything is all about you, and acting in accordance with that belief. The farther you follow a path that is all about you, the farther you will stray from your goals. In contrast, the sooner you surrender your life to God's higher purpose and accept your own blessed role within that purpose, the more personal happiness and abundance you will receive.

While I'm guessing that very few of us would ever say that we believe ourselves to be greater than God, the fact is that many of us still behave as if we *do* believe that. We pass judgment where we have no right to; we get complacent and comfortable and therefore spiritually lazy, forgetting that God provided for us so that we might carry out our work in his name; we abuse ourselves through excess or addiction, forgetting that our bodies are temples to use in service; we focus on money and material wealth as a primary—or even sole—goal of our lives.

How can we allow God to fill our lives if our lives are too full of ourselves?

Disproportionate self-love, which includes vanity, separates us from God and our fellow man. It thereby becomes the seed from which the other sins flourish.

Ego is at the heart of *anger* when we rail against those who do not acknowledge our power or importance.

Ego is at the heart of *envy* when we believe that we are more deserving than another or wish to see another fail to make us feel better.

Ego is at the heart of *complacency* when we don't take action to further God's plan or help others because we aren't willing to disrupt our personal comfort.

Ego is at the heart of *greed* when we feel we are entitled to hoard more than our share and to take from others, and when we value money or power over God.

Ego is at the heart of *indulgence* when we disrespect our body, mind, and spirit through excess or abuse.

Ego is at the heart of *lust* when we objectify another human being for the sole purpose of our physical pleasure.

The faster you get out of your own way, the faster you can experience divine fulfillment and abundance. If you are following this prayer practice faithfully, your efforts in the first three petals of faith, surrender, and service will ensure that you are operating in a place of selflessness rather than a place of ego. A regular prayer practice is like taking vitamins and exercising: it is preventive medicine that keeps you from falling victim to the other sins that will make you spiritually ill.

ANGER
(SOMETIMES LISTED AS WRATH OR IRE)

I think, for most of us, anger is the most common and the toughest of the patterns of evil thought to conquer. It certainly has been for me. My constant challenge is to live each day with as much love as I can, to love my neighbor as myself. Some days that's very easy to do. Others, not so much. As a deeply flawed inhabitant of God's earth, I have struggled with all these "patterns of evil thought" just as you likely have. But anger is my nemesis, and I have to work on it consciously—and often. A lot of things make me mad in this world, and I have a hard time keeping that reaction in check. Things like injustice, intolerance, bigotry, and apathy make me very angry. But sometimes it's the little things that send us over the edge: bad service in a restaurant, the politics of Little League baseball, parent-teacher meetings, annoying coworkers, disrespectful teenagers, and rush hour traffic.

Yet I found inspiration recently, in a most unlikely place, that helped me to work with the energy of anger in a creative way.

I came across an interview with Bob Geldof, the acerbic Irish rock star who has dedicated much of his career to the cause of ending global poverty. He is a fearless and outspoken man of extraordinary character, whose work and commitment inspires people all over the world. As for his personality and temperament . . . well, Mother Teresa he's not. Bob Geldof is angry, and he admits it.

In the interview, Sir Bob, discussing the idea of activism, described a primary difference between himself and his friend Bono, another Irish rocker who has dedicated admirable time and effort toward changing the world for the better. Geldof said, "Bono, as we all know, is in love with the world. He's enamored by it. I'm enraged by it. He wants to give the world a great big hug; I want to punch its lights out."

That quote made me laugh at first, but then I started really thinking about it and came to the conclusion that it was pure genius because it represents a great human conundrum: how, exactly, are those of us who are trying to embrace a philosophy of love supposed to deal with our anger over the injustices that drive us to the brink? We all wrestle with our anger over the issues in our own lives as well as out there in the world. How do we keep that anger from bubbling over?

The lesson I took from looking at Geldof's example was this:

> *Anger is a powerful emotion,*
> *and when anger is channeled properly,*
> *it can be an irresistible force used to positive affect.*

Rather than simply ranting at the world—or worse, allowing the anger to devour our insides when we suppress it—we need to find constructive ways to harness that energy and put it to work for change. Bob Geldof motivated a majority of the entire entertainment industry, and ultimately millions of global citizens, not only to care but to take action about the plight of suffering human beings. He did this by harnessing his anger—and making it work in a dynamic way.

And what happens when we look to Jesus for examples on anger? What emotion was Jesus displaying when he turned over the moneylenders' and merchants' tables in the Temple? This was a violent act of vandalism. Jesus must have been angry when he did it.

Is it possible that the Prince of Peace sometimes wanted to punch the world's lights out too? In turning over the tables, Jesus was taking a stand against those who he felt had turned a place of spirituality into a marketplace of iniquity. His anger was a righteous indignation that moved him into action. But his anger also caused a lot of trouble for him with the authorities in Jerusalem.

Perhaps Jesus tried to show us his humanity in the story of the Temple tables, so that we could relate to him that much more. If even Jesus lost his temper at times, perhaps we shouldn't be too hard on ourselves about our imperfections. Anger is a most difficult demon to tame. But in the interest of living with more love and changing the world, channeling it into a force for justice or charity seems a most effective means of dealing with it.

You don't have to be an activist to apply this idea. You can use it in your own life for your own benefit as well, which is a perfectly acceptable and very positive thing to do. Think about how much adrenaline builds inside you when you are angry about something. You know, that feeling that you want to explode when something or someone has really ticked you off? What if you could take that same energy and reroute it, use it toward a personal goal that you may have?

Exercise: **How Angry Are You?**

- Make a list of everything that has made you angry in the last week.
- Add any issue, global or otherwise, that makes you angry when you think about it.
- Can you channel the energy of anger that you feel over any of these issues into some kind of positive force or peaceful action that helps you to release the anger?
- If not, can you diminish the anger through the process of forgiveness as you learned it in the previous chapter? If your anger is triggered by a person's actions, can you use the affirmation *People are doing the best they can with what they have* and move on?

ENVY

Envy is potentially the most toxic of the sins. Envy corrodes the soul and rusts the heart, turning love and joy into bitterness. Envy is jealousy on steroids. It is the desire to see someone else fail. It is wishing ill on your fellow men, because they have something that you do not. Envy is offensive to God, for it shows a desperate lack of faith in his power to provide. When we suffer from envy, we resent that another has been given something that we wish we had. Perhaps we even feel that that person was given something that was rightly ours. If you believe that God's power is unlimited, then you must also know that he is capable of providing plenty for all his children. God does not play favorites, he does not have "pets." His is a very just system. Anytime you feel that you have been slighted, try this affirmation:

> *We live in a just universe, created by a just and loving God who treats all his children equally. There is plenty to go around, and mine is coming!*

That's a good affirmation to use when you start to hear the footfalls of the little green monster. Envy is truly an "evil thought," yet with a little work it is also completely avoidable.

If you lose something to another, no matter what it is—a promotion, a boyfriend, an auction, a contest, anything—it just means that your own path is different from the one you may have imagined. Your dreams will manifest differently, and ultimately in a way that is perfectly in harmony with your own destiny. But also remember that you have created that path by your thoughts and actions. Learn to trust divine intelligence in these circumstances, but check yourself as well. If you are feeling any envy toward another, you will cripple your own ability to attract abundance to yourself. The more bitter the envy, the more damage you do to your own spirit.

Remember that in the chapter on forgiveness you learned that *no one can steal your destiny.* This is a big world with a lot of work to be done, so some of us are going to have similar missions. Therefore the fact that someone gains something that you want does not mean that you have been excluded from ever having that desire. It simply means that you are on similar paths. Rather than resenting someone for sharing your destiny, learn to embrace that person as your brother or sister on the path.

Envy can also be the by-product of judgment. You may think that other people's success is unfair, that they don't deserve it based on what you have observed of their behavior. But that is for God alone to judge. You can't see inside their souls, but God can. He knows their pasts and he knows their intentions, which is vital information that you do not have. So rather than expending so much energy on what others have and why you think they don't deserve it (which brings into play that root sin, ego), you can change your life by taking that same energy and refocusing it on what you can be doing to make your own life better.

As for envy in personal and romantic relationships, the feeling you have when someone else is dating or involved with the object of your affection can be a very intense and corrosive form of envy. While we will look at love (and the secret of how to attract the real thing) in the next chapter, we must deal with envy here if it is an issue for you. For the sake of your own heart, health, and happiness, you must heal this kind of jealousy as quickly as you can. If you have "lost in love," it is because you were not with the right person, and God is trying to help you by making you available to a true soul mate who awaits you. Someone truly better for you is out there, and you must hold fast to your faith and trust that. Try this affirmation if you need it:

True love cannot be stolen. The right mate is out there for me and will come into my life as soon as I am ready.

You must be prepared to release with love and forgiveness those who have hurt you. Keep the lessons of the relationship by holding on to the understanding that every breakup and each perceived rejection gives you an opportunity to move forward through understanding what works in our lives and what does not.

> *Rejection is God's gift to you;*
> *it is his way of telling you that you are on the wrong track*
> *and need to move in another direction.*

Rejection is the doorway that allows envy to enter. Although rejection never feels good, it gets much easier to accept and you will heal far faster once you have surrendered to it as a gift from God. This principle applies to rejection on all levels: personal, romantic, business, creative. Remember the simple surrender affirmation:

> *If you believe that everything happens for a reason, you will never have a bad day.*

Exercise: **What Turns You Green with Envy?**

- Think about a time when you were consumed by envy over someone else's success. It can be business or personal.
- Now answer these questions: Why do I feel this way? Do I want what he or she has? Do I feel like I deserve it more? Do I feel like I somehow cannot have what I want because someone else has received it? Would it make me feel better to see him lose what he has? Be honest!
- Do you resent the person, or just the achievement? Usually the two are inseparable, but not always. Sometimes we really like someone— a coworker for example—but are envious when he or she is given

something we want. Can you turn that emotion around and be happy for that person's success, knowing definitively now that *he or she has not taken anything away from you?*

No one brings to this world what you do. No one can replace you. No one can steal your destiny. And there is plenty to go around. You do not ever need to be envious of others. Their success enhances yours; it does not diminish it. Allow them their joy, their success, and their glory, knowing that the more you celebrate the happiness of your brothers and sisters on earth, the happier you will be.

COMPLACENCY
(SOMETIMES LISTED AS SLOTH)

I don't use the antiquated term *sloth* because it sounds too much like a cute little three-toed creature that you'd find in the rain forest (the slow-moving mammal was, in fact, named after the sin). But there is nothing at all endearing about this sloth. It is a very dangerous "pattern of thought" that must be addressed seriously. In modern times we call it complacency, apathy, or indifference.

Many traditional treatises on the seven deadly sins refer to it as such. And laziness can definitely be hazardous to your spiritual health and physical well-being. Inertia is inaction, and neither of those states is going to lead anyone to change his or her life, much less the world. But there is a larger, more disturbing issue that underlies this seemingly not-such-a-big-deal sin.

In *The Divine Comedy*, Dante defines sloth as the failure to fulfill the primary commandment, which is to "love God with all one's heart, all one's mind, and all one's soul."

Ah, now we're onto something important. Dante was spot-on when he linked sloth to this primary commandment, which appears in several places in the New Testament, including Mark 12 and Luke 10, and in numerous passages of Hebrew scripture, most notably Deuteronomy 6. Sloth, laziness, indifference, inertia, whatever word you choose—all represent a lack of faith and a subsequent inability to show love and surrender to God. When we are apathetic about the world around us, we are not caring about God's plan, nor are we honoring our promise to create heaven on earth. We are not utilizing our talents in any active way to further our lives, and certainly not in the service-oriented way that God wishes for us.

When I share this prayer process, one of the questions I am asked often is "Do other people have the same promise and the same mission that I have?" It took me years of meditation, observation, and learning to understand it, but I have come to the solid conclusion that the only answer is yes. A number of people will have the *identical* mission, and many more will share *similar* missions. The reason is twofold. First, there is a great deal of work to do on a very large planet, so we need many people committed to doing the same job. The second and more urgent reason is that *not everyone will fulfill their destinies and keep their promises*. This forces the workload to fall heavier on the shoulders of those who do keep their promises, because there are fewer to carry the burden. Ego and complacency are the two sins that will undermine our "reason for being" over and over, if we allow them to creep in and take hold.

Sad, isn't it? The evil patterns of apathy and complacency threaten to keep us from happiness and prevent us from feeling the love of God through our service to him and his beautiful earth. If that's not terrible enough, complacency forces our brothers and sisters on earth to work that much harder to pick up the slack. Thank the Lord that there are people on this planet who are willing to do so much more than their share and are working that much harder.

I have a wonderful and inspirational friend, Sarah Symons, who is the founder of the Emancipation Network, an organization that fights the evils of human trafficking and provides services and resources to survivors of slavery. Sarah gave up her career in music and film to dedicate her life to this cause. The more she became aware of the horrors that exist worldwide, of women and children forced into sexual slavery by the *millions*, the more she knew that she could no longer live a life that was not committed to service and activism. Sarah works tirelessly to make an impact on this terrible and overwhelming global plague. She personally is responsible for helping hundreds of women around the world. And yet Sarah doesn't sleep at night, because she is constantly trying to find ways to expand her commitment, to help even more people.

My point is that Sarah would get some sleep if more people cared about this issue and carried their weight in the service department. She has to help hundreds, and strives to help thousands more, because not enough people are doing their share! If everyone fulfilled their promises and became truly committed to service, the burden of labor would be a little more equal and an awful lot lighter.

This sin is committed by people who cannot bother to care. Recently at a local community gathering, I mentioned the plight of an elderly friend while speaking with another guest. The man I was chatting with was someone I was meeting for the first time, but ours is a very service-oriented community, so I assumed that he shared similar values. I explained that I was concerned about this friend as she is a frail, tiny woman who cleans houses for a living. Her husband is terminally ill, and she can no longer make ends meet. She's also exhausted from her trips to the hospital and then back to work in a physically taxing job. I posed the question, "How do we best help her, and how do we help so many in our community who are like her and hurting in this economy?"

The man stared at me blankly, as if the question had been asked in some exotic foreign language. Finally, his response before walking away from me—quickly—was "People are poor because they didn't work hard enough. It's their fault. And it's not my responsibility to bail them out."

Oh my.

I was speechless at the callousness, at the apathy, and at the ego. But after I got over the shock, I actually felt sorry for him. This man had sealed his own fate with his harsh disregard for the neighbors that he has been charged to love. I knew at that moment that he would be confronted with challenges as a result of his hardened heart, possibly very painful challenges. I don't wish that on anyone, but we are here to learn and God can be a tough headmaster when his students aren't listening. It has been my observation that those who show the highest degree of apathy and complacency get hit with the harshest lessons. They are lessons we signed up for. When we understand why we are here and what is expected of us—which according to Jesus is to show compassion and love toward one another—our lives are harmonious and beautiful. When we forget that all-important commandment for too long, our lives will be realigned with a lesson of clarity.

Let me stress that a lot of really good people are victims of this behavior pattern. I know a number of very successful, decent, family-oriented men and women who are also guilty of apathy. They believe that as long as they provide for themselves and their family, they have done the job they are here to do. They take their success as their due. They worked hard; they earned their money; they should be able to do whatever they want with it. Right?

Well, yes. And . . . no.

Yes, we should all have the freedom of enjoying the fruits of our labors. Remember that God loves us and wants us to be happy! But God grants us opportunities and even riches because he is counting on us to contribute to his human family; he is relying on us to give to charity and to seek out ways to serve our fellow man as a means of expressing our gratitude. The more successful you are financially, the more obligated you are to make a difference. So when you pray for unlimited abundance, keep this in mind at all times:

> *If you are put in a position of power, wealth, or fame,*
> *it is because God is trusting you to use that authority and influence wisely*
> *and to the benefit of your brothers and sisters.*
> *There is no way around this!*

Now, more than ever, with the crises that face this planet and its people, we need all hands on deck. Everyone who has the capacity to serve must do so. Anything less is disdainful of the great gifts that God has bestowed upon us.

Among some truly inspirational quotes from historical figures about this issue, my favorite is credited to an eighteenth-century British statesman, Edmund Burke, who said, "All that is necessary for evil to triumph is for good men to do nothing." It's brilliant and cohesive, encapsulating as it does the entire problem of complacency in a single sentence. You may be a good person, but if you do nothing to better the planet, you are allowing the triumph of evil. And Eleanor Roosevelt said, "So much attention is paid to the aggressive sins, such as violence and cruelty and greed with all their tragic effects, that too little attention is paid to the passive sins, such as apathy and laziness, which in the long run can have a more devastating effect."

To put it more simply, if you're not part of the solution, you're part of the problem. And the more blessed you have been by God, the more you need to care about those who are less fortunate than you. Complacency is a high spiritual crime. It is an affront against God, against your fellow humans, and against yourself. If you are fortunate enough to have a comfortable life, but you are not spiritually committed enough to use that life to make the world a better place, you can expect to answer for your failure sooner or later. Nature abhors a vacuum, and God is likewise unhappy with vacuous behavior from his children, particularly the children he has cared for and rewarded so generously. Here is a cautionary tale that I hope will help you to see this issue clearly.

Many years ago, when I was still a fledgling on my spiritual path, I had the opportunity to work on a project with a wealthy man. Or perhaps I should say that I *nearly* had the opportunity. I was part of a proposed charitable project that would have raised funds and consciousness for some urgent global issues. Now, the entire project was built around this particular celebrity and could not be accomplished without his participation. Originally, he had been excited and interested in the idea, just long enough for some of us to spend time and energy—a lot of time and energy—to try to make it happen. But at the last minute, our golden boy changed his mind and simply couldn't be bothered with it.

He explained to me, quite sweetly really, that while he knew it was a great project and knew that his input was vital to make it happen, this was simply a bad time for him to do anything charitable. Why? *Because he didn't feel like it.* He was enjoying his highly privileged and completely carefree lifestyle at the moment and he wasn't really all that pushed to do anything else, particularly when that something else was starting to sound like a lot like work. Not only did he bail out of the project, he bailed out on all of us involved, never again returning any of our calls, despite the fact that we had referred to each other as "friend" for quite some time. All of us involved were hurt deeply—personally, professionally, and financially—by his actions.

But there's more to this story. Much more. It is not for me or anyone else to determine what is or is not enough for each person to give back to his or her community or the planet. That is an issue between each individual and God. However, this man placed that judgment on himself. *He told me at the time that he knew his decision was wrong.* He said that he knew he should be doing more service work, that he knew he had been blessed with extraordinary good fortune, and that maybe "one day" he would dedicate more time to humanitarian issues. But not now.

Can you guess what happened? That man's life took a drastic, downward turn. Everything that allowed him to live his carefree, opulent, privileged lifestyle was suddenly and harshly taken from him in a most shocking way. He was hit by the divine two-by-four. Hard. He never saw it coming, and he reeled for years.

But while this tale is about his behavior, it's equally about my reaction. I confess, much as it hurts me to admit, that I gloated over his misfortune. I cheered the laws of karma for catching up to him. "Serves him right," I said. *Ugh.* It pains me to write that even now. Please eliminate that ugly and judgmental phrase from your vocabulary for the rest of your life. Back then, I had so much to learn about forgiveness. I carried anger and resentment over that man and that situation for many, many years. What a waste! My feelings didn't impact him one way or another; they only damaged me. Now I realize that this experience was really my opportunity to find forgiveness. We can and must pray for the people around us whom we see entrapped by complacency. In the same way, I also pray for our neighbor who thinks that all poor people created their own plight and should be abandoned to their misery.

And therein lies another law of forgiveness:

> *If you believe that someone you know*
> *is behaving in a way that may be harmful to himself or others,*
> *you have an obligation to pray for him.*

This law is not about passing judgment or infringing upon someone else's free will. You are simply praying that this person will gently find his connection to God and fulfill his own promise. The rest is out of your hands. How he does that is really none of your business. But this type of prayer, toward someone else's highest good and happiness, is extremely effective. It has the power to save another human being from experiencing something truly terrible, and the whole world benefits each time someone awakens to his higher purpose.

This is part of your service commitment. It is part of everyone's promise to bring about a more peaceful and harmonious earth through forgiveness and loving thought, even toward those who hurt us. Especially toward those who hurt us.

Generosity Is the Antidote to Complacency

While finishing this book, I saw a story on a news channel that made me weep, first with sadness and then with joy and relief. A woman in Texas sat on the floor of a Dallas auction house, sobbing almost uncontrollably. Her name was Tracy, and her home was in foreclosure and was going up on the block. She had come to the auction because she was still unable to believe that her family was about to lose everything. Perhaps the auction would give her some kind of closure.

As Tracy cried, a woman she had never seen or met, named Marilyn, walked through the auction house. She was in search of her son, who was there to buy a foreclosed property. Marilyn stopped when she saw Tracy, unable to walk past another human being in so much pain, and asked her why she was so distraught. Tracy told her. And when Tracy's house came up for auction, Marilyn bid on it. And bid again, and bid again. She had never seen the house, there was no photo of it in the auction catalog, and she had no idea what its value was on the market. But she knew what its value was to the sobbing Tracy, and she bid until she won.

Marilyn gave Tracy—a perfect stranger—her house back. She spent $30,000 of her own money to save the home of a family she did not know. When asked why she did it, Marilyn seemed taken aback by the question before she remarked, "Wouldn't everybody?"

It was Marilyn's response to that question that made me cry the hardest. She helped Tracy *because she could*. Simple. And in her sincere kindness and compassion, Marilyn truly believes that everyone with the capacity to do the same would do the same. Marilyn's reality is the reality God wants for the world—that we would all help each other in such a way because it is what we are here to do. It is what God wants for all of us.

Marilyn's example provides us with the antidote for complacency. And with her actions, she created a miracle for Tracy!

Exercise: **Are You Now or Have You Ever Been Complacent?**

- Considering the cited examples, have you ever "begged off" of a project because it was just too much work—even if you knew it was important? When and why?

- Have you ever felt guilty that you weren't doing enough to help others who are less fortunate than you? Give an example if the answer is yes.

- Have you ever said—or thought—that poor people have created their own plight? Or that someone else's tragedy is "not my problem"?

- Do you feel differently after working through this prayer practice and realizing your larger place in God's plan?

- How do you think that your own happiness and opportunity are tied to your actions toward other people?

- Whom can you pray for today that may be suffering from complacency?

- If you were in the position to help a perfect stranger as Marilyn did in the story above, would you do it? Why or why not?

GREED
(SOMETIMES LISTED AS AVARICE)

Greed is the opposite of generosity, but it is more than the unwillingness to share abundance. It is also the willingness to forgo other virtues—like honesty and integrity—in order to gain wealth or material goods. You don't have to be rich to be greedy. People who are unwilling to give of themselves are greedy.

Jesus tells us in Matthew 6:24: *"No one can serve two masters, because either he will hate one and love the other, or be loyal to one and despise the other. You cannot serve God and Mammon."*

Mammon is sometimes interpreted as *money*, but that is too narrow a definition. *Mammon*, as it appears in the Bible, comes from an Aramaic origin that has a more complex meaning. In this case, *Mammon* refers to all manner of material or worldly goods or pleasures. Anytime we view any of those things as more important than fulfilling our basic promises to God and to each other, we are at risk for being greedy. When we define our success in terms of material wealth, we are not only missing the point, we are often falling into a truly perilous trap.

But It's Just Business . . .

Valuing material objects above God and working to get those things at the expense of someone else's happiness or security is one of the darkest patterns of evil thought. It harms everyone and dims the light in the world. And don't think that referring to the relentless pursuit of material goods as "business" erases any responsibility you have to behave in a humane way. How many times have you heard something explained away with the phrase "It's just business," as if those are magic words that erase transgressions and make odious behavior acceptable?

Do you think God cares about semantics
when humans damage each other and cause each other tremendous pain?

I once worked for a corporate giant where a young man shot himself in his office because of the way he was treated at work. I can assure you that his widow and young children would not be consoled by knowing that what caused his despair was "just business." It's a rough example, but a necessary one. I'm sure Wall Street has many more cautionary tales such as this. Hurting another human being under the guise of business is reprehensible, yet it happens every day in thousands of different ways. Maybe millions of ways. Usually the ubiquitous "It's just business" is followed by "nothing personal." How ridiculous it is to believe that anything that causes another to suffer isn't "personal." All pain is personal.

What would happen if we stopped compartmentalizing our relationships, if we stopped hiding behind definitions that we have invented to excuse our unspiritual behavior on a daily basis? What if we no longer had *business relationships* and instead referred to all our interactions simply as *human relationships*. What if we truly treated everyone the way that we wish to be treated all the time, regardless of the circumstances? The world as we know it could transform with that simple approach to our day-to-day living.

Greed Is the Root of Evil

We hear the old adage "Money is the root of all evil." This isn't really true, and money can be the root of some very great initiatives toward peace and beauty and goodness. Thus I would rewrite that phrase as "Greed is the root of much evil." And greed comes in a number of forms.

Greed for power is as egregious as greed for money. How many political campaigns have dissolved into horrific and hard-to-watch mudslinging contests where candidates will do absolutely anything to get elected? That kind of behavior falls under the category of greed, and it is as common in politics as it is in business. I shudder at what some of these candidates have invited upon themselves by their behavior. Lying and smearing another just to gain an office is most definitely the result of a pattern of evil thought. It diminishes everyone and pulls entire nations into the mire of such low behavior.

Exercise: **Greed in the Day-to-Day Business of Our Lives**

Greed is a harsh sin, and one that occurs in varying degrees. You can be a very decent person and still come under the seductive spell of greed.

- Have you ever done something dishonest to gain in business, such as cheating a coworker or client, overcharging someone because you could get away with it, or lying to make a sale? Have you ever lied or smeared another to ensure your own promotion?

- Have you ever used the excuse "It's just business" or "It's nothing personal"? Do you think you will ever use it again?

- If the answer to the above question is yes, take a vow here and now to change that approach for your own spiritual well-being. *Decide that you will never again fall back on the idea that business transactions allow you to suspend your humanity.*

- Think back to a time when you were harsh toward another in business. Now imagine Jesus, as God's representative, sitting in the room with you. Would you be able to make the same decisions? Say the same things? If you think on a regular basis of Jesus sitting next to you while you are working, how will your behavior change?

If you think it is ever acceptable to exploit another human being for any reason, you are headed for a hard fall. No one gets away with it. No one. And such behavior thwarts your own happiness and abundance. Even if you think you won that particular match and got what you wanted, you will eventually lose the game. And of course, the truth is that you don't need to hurt anyone else in order to have extraordinary wealth. In fact, the opposite is true! You will be given far more than you can imagine when you respond with love, generosity, and grace to your fellow humans. Remember, they are your brothers and sisters on earth, and they are God's children.

I will leave you to meditate on greed with the definitive question that Jesus asks us in Matthew 16, verse 26:

"What good will it be for a man if he gains the whole world, yet forfeits his soul?"

INDULGENCE
(SOMETIMES LISTED AS GLUTTONY)

In medieval times when the seven sins were listed, *indulgence* was often called *gluttony*, referring primarily to overeating. And while the word *gluttony* evolved from a Latin root that means "to gulp," that definition doesn't really illustrate this particular pattern of evil thought accurately or thoroughly. Gluttony was symbolic of the wealthy person who gorged on rich foods while the poor suffered and scrounged for bread. Imagine spending hundreds of dollars an ounce on caviar, when you knew that your neighbors and their children hadn't eaten anything in a week, other than what they could scrounge from a rubbish heap. Your caviar allowance could have fed them for a year. That is gluttony. People who withheld aid from the poor when they had more than they needed were guilty of gluttonous behavior in Dante's medieval world. Certainly in an environment where famine is present and the stakes are human lives, overeating and hoarding food would be an obscenity.

In modern terms, indulgence is really the sin of excess. Let me just be very clear here, however. *There is absolutely nothing wrong with enjoying good food and reveling in the finer things in life.* I do not believe that God wants you to live the life of an ascetic and deprive yourself of comforts and pleasures. In fact, Jesus didn't believe this either, and it's something that landed him in trouble. Jesus was even called a glutton because he didn't subscribe to the ascetic lifestyle. He was also called a drunkard because he drank wine and dined with those who were considered "unclean" (Matthew 11:19 and Luke 7:34).

Of course, Jesus was neither a glutton nor a drunkard. Those terms were used to slander him by those who wanted to diminish the importance of his message. But the fact that he did not subscribe to the strict ascetic principles of his cousin, John the Baptist, is an indication that he didn't condemn the good life—as long as it was not one of excess and overindulgence.

In modern spiritual terms, indulgence means a lack of self-control, a love of excess, and an immersion into luxury over all else. In Hebrew, the word that we translate as "gluttony" is *zalel*, which means to be lavish and/or to squander. Let me give you a modern example of this kind of indulgence. I recently read an article in a woman's magazine about a British pop star who bragged about her collection of Hermès handbags, of which she allegedly owns over a hundred. Now, for the non-fashionistas who may not know what that means, let me explain that Hermès is a French luxury brand. Hermès bags of the style that the pop star collects range in price from seven thousand dollars at the low end, up to six figures each when they are constructed of exotic animal skins and have gold and diamond clasps. In other words, this woman's handbag collection—and this is just one particular brand that we know about—is worth potentially millions of dollars.

Is that excess? Is that indulgence? While you may want to scream, "Yes! Of course it is!" allow me to stop you. Here's the tricky part. It's not for us to judge her, because when we do that, we impose man-made standards on spiritual issues. Who then becomes the judge of what is too much? Who decides how many handbags one pop star can or should have? Who defines *lavish*? Who draws the line?

The answer is that this issue, as all others, is between each individual and God. We must all search our own conscience to make such a determination about what constitutes the sin of indulgence within the context of our own lives and behavior.

It is entirely possible that this particular pop star donates significant amounts to charity to offset her lavish spending on handbags. I honestly have no idea whether she is at all philanthropic or what is in her spirit. Nor do I know what it is in her psyche that motivates her to desire a purple ostrich purse that sells for fifty thousand dollars. But something does, and perhaps it is some deep-seated poverty or lack from her child-hood, some issue she has to work through on her own. If that is the case, I owe her compassion rather than judgment. Remember, *people are doing the best they can with what they have.* Even multimillionaire pop stars.

Now, to be perfectly honest, when I read this story, I immediately thought of how many people could be fed or given medical care or res-cued from slavery with even ten percent of the money she spends on each posh accessory. And I hope with all my heart that she thinks like that as well. But if she doesn't, then it is only a matter of time before she encounters a self-imposed lesson about the evils of excess for excess's sake. I'll be watching the headlines to see if this happens, but I won't revel in it if it does. Instead, I will pray that this woman realizes just how many human lives she can aid, or even save, if she decides to reevaluate her spending habits. That is a much more constructive use of my energy!

Exercise: **Are You a Glutton?**

- Do you have a weakness for some material item that causes you to overindulge? What is it? Addictive habits, like cigarettes and alco-hol, even gambling, are indulgences. Do you have a weakness for any of those? Do you spend a disproportionate amount of your income on any of those things?
- Have you recently felt guilty about overindulging in anything? What and why? If you feel guilt, you need to consider why you don't feel

right about your course of action.. How can you prevent that feeling in the future?

- What is the most extravagant and potentially indulgent thing you have ever done?

- Would you consider giving ten percent of your indulgent spending away to charity? You can still have luxury items and spend as freely as you wish. It's just a commitment to be aware and conscious as you indulge.

- Have you passed judgment on others for indulgent behavior? On whom and why? How do you feel differently—or not—about that point of view now?

What Is Your Attitude Toward Wealth?

Contemplating the sin of indulgence can teach you a lot about yourself and how you view wealth. For example, if you think the kind of excess described above is obscene and you are inclined to think negative thoughts about the very rich who behave in such a way, you may be doing yourself a tremendous disservice. If you believe that wealth is wicked, you will not be able to attract wealth to yourself. It is important that you realign that thinking. Money is a type of energy. You can and should make it work for you, for your loved ones, for your community, and for the world. When you move the energy in that direction, it not only increases, it comes back to you in even larger increments! Use this affirmation:

Wealth enables freedom and happiness. I am committed to using my forthcoming wealth with consciousness to create a beautiful life for myself and others.

Remember the story of my friend James who has a love of European sports cars? He bought his extravagant car and made a commitment to charity all at the same time; he feels great about having what makes him happy and helping the world. It is a very good compromise. In fact, he gives to charity in a way that he might not have if he hadn't bought the car, because buying it caused him to realign his thinking. I have done the same thing with fashion. True confessions: I have a weakness for French and Italian designers, but I hope my closet would not cause you to call me self-indulgent. I choose my expenditures carefully, and when I decide to splurge on a particular label, I always donate to charity to spread the good feelings!

Stay with me here because this is important. There is an interesting spiritual evolution that happens through practicing this philosophy of combining luxury with charity. *It forces you to consider what value you get for the money.*

This practice ultimately changed the way I think about those luxury items I used to covet. While I may still love the way a gorgeously crafted Dior bag looks, now that I know how far that same amount of money will go if donated to the antislavery movement, I don't really want to spend it on a handbag! Let me think . . . I can buy a purse or I can provide shelter, safety, and medical treatment for survivors who have been rescued from the horrors of human trafficking. For me, there is no contest anymore. The more immersed I become in global service endeavors, the less I want to spend money on extravagances like high-end fashion. Sure, I still gawk at the pages of the glossy magazines, and Chanel and Pucci make me sigh with their European elegance. But I simply don't need those things anymore. The euphoria I experience from knowing I am really making a difference in someone's life is far more satisfying to me than a great purse. So while no one will be modeling a *Sex and the City* character after me anytime soon, I'm really okay with that. I think I'll create my own show and call it *Service and the City*—an urban tale of fabulous fortysomething friends who auction off their designer duds and give the money to shelters for abused women and children.

Let me stress that this was my choice, my free will, to change the way I indulge myself. I arrived at the decision after using this prayer practice for quite some time. It doesn't mean I'll never buy a designer item again, it just means that I don't need them anymore, nor do I seek them out as I once did. But I pass no judgment on anyone else's desires. Instead, I offer this path to them with love that they may see where the journey takes them.

LUST

Our bodies are sacred receptacles for the spirit; they are the containers of all that we are and have promised to be. When we are joined with another human being in the act of love, we are combining our spirits through our bodies. It is a devotional act, a celebration of sacred union.

Lust, on the other hand, disconnects the body from the spirit. It is an act of animal attraction, a physical response devoid of humanity. It removes love from the act and therefore diminishes us. Sex without love means disrespecting our bodies, which are meant to be kept as temples; it means forgetting that union is divine and that it should not be entered into casually and without consciousness. If you are in a casual sexual relationship, you are not respecting your spirituality. When you participate in sexual acts with another, you are blending your spirit with another's, and another's with yours. This is a very serious commitment, and one that can and will impact every aspect of your life.

The Gnostic Gospels affirm that sex should be conducted only when both *trust* and *consciousness* are present.

Trust, in this context, suggests that the lovers have a real knowledge and caring for each other and know that each holds the other's highest good in his and her hearts. This leads to *consciousness,* which represents the spiritual understanding that sex is a sacred prospect, one that combines the life forces and essences of two people—and that it is a celebration of God's greatest gifts in the flesh.

Certainly, using this standard eliminates casual sex and one-night stands! Trust and consciousness are the result of having an authentic relationship. They do not come instantly. Therefore Jesus and his later followers were warning against sex without love. Jesus says in Matthew 5:28, "*But I say to you that whoever looks at a woman to lust for her has already committed adultery with her in his heart.*" Now if we look at the definition of lust as wanting to have sex without caring for the other person, without trust or consciousness, it gives us a new level of understanding. Jesus wasn't just saying, "Guard against your sexual impulses." He was saying, "Do not objectify and dehumanize another person by wanting him or her solely for sexual purposes."

Imagine the changes we could make in our world today if we could reinforce this principle, starting with teaching our young people to respect their own bodies and to honor each other as spiritual beings *first and foremost.* Lust is rampant in the media of the twenty-first century, and that media is often geared toward teenagers. Sex sells, and unfortunately it sells by demeaning human beings through presenting them as physical objects devoid of spirit. This objectification creates the climate that allows both violence against women and sexual exploitation as is found in human trafficking and sexual slavery.

Of course I am not saying that all sex without love leads to such extreme circumstances and even crime. But I am saying that if we were all raised to view sexuality as a sacrament, as the unification of two spirits through the coming together of their bodies, then maybe we would be well on our way to creating a new and healthier worldview.

Anyone who has ever had a one-night stand and awakened to regret it knows how awful that feels. Why? Because on some level you know that you have violated the divinity of your spirit by sharing your life force with someone without thought and, worse, without love. Lust is a selfish impulse, and once that impulse is satisfied, there is an emptiness left in its place. Lust does not know compassion. It is, in that regard, the opposite of love. You do not lust after someone you are in love with. Rather, you desire that person. You care about him or her and are conscious about what happens next.

Love is all about giving. Lust, on the other hand, is strictly about taking.

Finally, if God *is* love (and he is, as defined in John 4:8) and love cannot occupy the same space as lust, then we are by nature *completely removed from God when we are indulging in lust*. And why wouldn't we be? Do you really think that God wants to hang around and watch while we treat each other as objects with no spirit?

Exercise: **Lust versus Love**

- Think of a time when you felt lust for someone, a strictly physical or chemical attraction. Did you act upon that feeling? If so, how did you feel afterward?
- Does the idea of viewing sex as sacred union, as the blending of two spirits through the coming together of the bodies, change your perspective?

- What do you think it means to have trust and consciousness in the bedroom? Have you ever experienced that?

While no one is saying that you can't admire beauty or find someone you don't know to be physically attractive, it's what you do with those feelings that matters. And here's the really good news: sacred sexuality is a holy and euphoric gift from God. When such profound love is understood and embraced, empty and casual lust just seems tawdry and unworthy of the human experience. Lust demeans, love exalts. Which leads now out of the sixth petal and into the center of the rose, where pure love awaits us!

Whoever does not love
does not know God,
because God is love.

1 John 4:8

XI

The Center of the Rose—Love

L O V E

*T*he *Gnostic Gospel* of Philip states,

> *Love does not say "this is mine" but rather "this is yours."*

Love sits in the center of the rose because it is the heart of this prayer practice. Each repetition of this practice must be done with love in order to be truly effective.

> *Do all things with love and love will do all things.*

Your faith and surrender must come from your love for God, for yourself, and for your fellow humans. Your service commitments must be carried out with love, not strictly out of duty. You will attract more abundance in all aspects of your life as you become more loving, and forgiveness comes naturally when you live in love.

Evil does not exist in a place where love is strong.

WHAT IS THE DEFINITION OF LOVE?

Defining love is an enormous and daunting task, but attempting to understand the true nature of it is, I think, a noble effort. I discovered in my medieval prayer studies that early Gnostic Christians believed that love was *present in six aspects of expression.* I found in studying these that I learned a lot more about the nature of love than I had dreamed possible:

Agape—This is the word most often translated in the gospels simply as "love." It is a spiritual love, the way God loves us. It is a love that is filled with the joy we find in each other and the world, the purest form of spiritual expression; most of all, it is unconditional and what we should all aspire to. This is the "highest love."

Philia—This is sometimes referred to as brotherly love (the city of *Phila*delphia is the "city of brotherly love"). It is the love found in friendship but also the love of blood siblings and true companions. It is a more mortal love in comparison with the spiritual transcendent nature of *agape*. An interesting letter from the apostle Peter tells us (1 Peter 1:22) that God wants us to demonstrate both. Note that this quote is translated most often with the word "love" occurring twice as it does here:

Now that you have obeyed the truth and have purified your souls to love your brothers sincerely, you must love *one another intensely and with a pure heart.*

In the original Greek, the first "love" is actually *philia* and the second "love" is *agape*. This is one of those issues where the English translation is a challenge, as we only have one word for love, whereas the ancients had many! So Saint Peter is telling us here that we must love our brothers and sisters sincerely first in our mortal way, and upon perfecting that, we must move to the next level, of loving them in imitation of God's unconditional approach. Love is an evolution. It grows and expands. In the Gospel of Thomas, Jesus tells us *"You must love your brother like your own soul,"* which is similar to what Peter is charging us to do.

Charis—This is a love that is defined by grace, devotion, and praise for God; this is where the love of our mother and father is found, on earth and in heaven. *Charis* means both "grace" and "kindness" in the original Greek. It is one of the two kinds of love that informs *service* and forms the root of the word *charity*. *Charis* describes nurturing, service that comes directly from the heart. It is also the love most present when we work through *forgiveness*.

Eunoia—Greek for "beautiful thinking," this is the love that inspires deep compassion and a commitment to the service of the world and all God's people; this is where our love for charity in our community lies, combining our hearts with our minds and putting them into motion. It is the other of the two kinds of love that informs *service*. This is love in action. *Eunoia* describes activism, service from the stimulated mind and the inspired heart.

Storge—"Affection" in Greek, *storge* is a pure love that is full of tenderness, caring, and empathy. This is where the love of children is found. It is innocent, playful, and sweet. *Storge* can also describe the love that we feel for our pets.

Eros—Representing romantic love but also sexual love when it is sacred, *eros* is a profound physical celebration in which the souls come together in the union of the bodies.

> *There is no darkness that cannot be defeated*
> *by the light of love in one of these expressions.*
> *When all are present in harmony*
> *Evil cannot exist at all.*

Exercise: **Six Types of Love**

- Go through the list of the six expressions of love, and cite examples of how each works in your life.
- Why do you think the ancients were careful to look at love from different angles and use different words to describe it? Does knowing these words change your own definition of what love is?

THE SOLUTION TO ALL PROBLEMS: LOVE MORE

One of the most simple, yet stunning and significant teachings I encountered in my study of the medieval Chartres principles came from this lesson about love:

> *There is no problem*
> *for which the instruction to* love more
> *is not the solution.*

I remember the first week that I was challenged by a teacher to do this in every situation that I encountered. No matter what or whom I was confronted with, I was given the instruction to love them more. Let me just tell you, this is hard. And if you don't believe me, try this exercise.

Exercise: **Learning to Love More!**

- Choose one day, preferably a business day or one when you know you will encounter many people with a variety of different personalities. Take a vow that from the moment you wake up to the time your head hits the pillow that night, your approach to every single situation that confronts you will be to love more. This applies to everyone you encounter: family, friends, coworkers, bosses, strangers, grocery clerks. Everyone. No matter how unpleasant they may be to you.

- At the end of the day, stop and think about every encounter, and ask yourself if you approached that situation with love. Could you have shown more love? Did you fail in certain circumstances or were you able to love more for the entire day?

- Think of the six kinds of love defined by the ancient mystery school and how they apply to the encounters you had during the day.

- Did you tell anyone that you were going to do this experiment, or did you keep it a secret? There are no rules about this; however, if you tell people, they will become curious and may decide to join you on your quest!

- When you have completed a full day successfully, take a pledge to attempt the same experiment for an entire week.

- When you have completed a week, continue to expand. The goal is to think like this every day, or at least as frequently as you can.

I found the results of this exercise stunning. Little things that would normally irritate me or cause me to snap or respond sarcastically didn't bother me a bit. I found that loving more most often felt like forgiveness. *People are doing the best they can with what they have*, I reminded myself often. I found that if I responded to someone with love and kindness, even when they didn't want it or expect it, my response transformed the energy of the exchange completely.

Charis, love that is graceful and kind, is the love we feel when we make the determination to *love more* in our day-to-day lives. This parable is my favorite illustration of that kind of love in action, but beyond this, it is a final exam of sorts. See how many lessons from all the preceding chapters you can find throughout this story.

THE PARABLE OF THE FISH IN THE LAKE

A young man who loved to go fishing read an advertisement in a glossy magazine about a sparkling lake where enormous rainbow trout leapt from the water. The advertisement indicated that the fish were so abundant and willing, they practically caught themselves. Excited by the prospect, he packed up his fishing gear and headed off on his journey, ultimately pitching a tent on the lakeshore. For several days he cast his fishing lines into the lake, but there were no bites on the bait and no sign of fish. There were no magical rainbow trout, leaping or otherwise. He grew frustrated, yet he stayed on the lakeshore, certain that if he just waited long enough, the fish would begin to pour in. After all, he had read about it in a shiny publication full of pretty pictures, and therefore it must be true.

Unbeknownst to the young fisherman, a wise grandmother who was the guardian of the lake had been watching him. After witnessing the young man's frustration for three full days, the wise one came down from her little ramshackle house on the hill and addressed the young man.

"My son, I have allowed you three days to come to this conclusion on your own, but now it is time somebody told you. There are no fish in that lake."

The young man was taken aback momentarily but merely laughed at the old woman. "But of course there are fish in that lake! I read it in the glossy magazine and therefore it must be true. I just haven't found my lucky streak yet."

The elder shook her head and repeated, "No. I have lived on these shores all my long life. There is not now, nor has there ever been, a fish in that lake."

With an impatient wave, the young fisherman dismissed the elder as a crazy old lady and returned to his task with renewed determination. Besides, she was a woman, and what did women know about fishing?

Shaking her head sadly, the old one retreated to her little home on the hill. She had seen this before, so many times. No doubt she would see it over and over again for as long as she lived.

Periodically the young man convinced himself that he saw one of the lines bob in the water out of the corner of his eye. A bite! There were fish in the lake! But a moment later, the surface of the water was still and he was forced to accept that the perceived bite was an illusion.

After a full week of casting his lines and becoming increasingly frustrated by the lack of fish, the young man packed his gear with a sigh. Maybe the old woman had been right. Maybe he should have listened to her. But he had not, and in addition to wasting a week of his life, he had come down with a terrible cold and had sat in poison ivy, which covered his body in a painful rash. He had pierced his fingers on the fishhooks several times in his frustration. It was well past time to go home.

As the young fisherman left the lake and began to climb the hill, he saw two enthusiastic young men setting up their fishing poles nearby on the lakeshore. Feeling like he had a responsibility to tell the truth as he had learned it the hard way, he approached the newcomers. "My friends," he began, "I hate to be the bearer of bad news, but I am here to tell you before you waste your time and end up ill and bleeding, as I have, that there are no fish in this lake."

The two young arrivals laughed out loud. Of course there were fish in this lake! Hadn't they read all about it?

"I'm telling you the truth. I have been here twenty-four hours a day for a full week and have yet to see evidence of even one fish in this lake." He pointed to the little house on the hill. "See up there? An old woman who has lived on the lakeshore all her life told me that there have never been fish in this lake."

The newcomers looked at each other and rolled their eyes, to indicate that they knew that this man, with his notions of no fish, was crazy. Or perhaps he was just a very bad fisherman. Clearly they were more talented and more determined and would certainly be successful in their search for the fish, where those who came before them had not been.

The first fisherman, wiser now, left them to it and decided to visit the grandmother before abandoning the lakeshore. She welcomed him in warmly.

"I'm sorry I didn't believe you," he said. "You are free to say 'I told you so' and to gloat about my foolishness."

The old woman shook her head. "No, my son. Your pain brings me no joy. I told you that there were no fish in the lake not for my own purposes but for yours. I hoped to save you from the pain that I have watched others experience over and over again. And I didn't expect you to listen to me, as it is the rare soul who ever does."

The fisherman thought about this for a moment before asking, "Why do you think that is?"

The elder began to sort through a first aid kit. She provided soothing medicine for the young man's rash and bandages for his wounded fingers as she explained patiently, "Because more often than not, you cannot save a person from experiencing their necessary lessons. Perhaps it is true that wisdom has no shortcuts. But it is also true that younger egos do not recognize elder experience as wisdom anymore. And so, while I will take pity on the young fishermen who come here and will advise them that there are no fish in the lake, it is entirely up to them to determine whether or not they believe me. But I am an old and poor woman who lives in a shack, and why should they believe me? I have nothing of value, therefore I am not worth listening to. And yet . . . I pray for them, all of them, just as I prayed for you. I pray that their lessons will not be too harsh or too painful. It is the one thing I can do to help them."

The two of them moved to the window at the front of the shack and watched the latest arrivals cast their lines and wait. "Will you tell them as you told me?" the first fisherman asked.

The old woman nodded. "Yes, of course I will. I always do. For you see, it is my job, it is why I live here on the lake. If I can save even one from wasting time and feeling pain, then I have accomplished my mission. And if I cannot, I must respect their need to experience the lesson. Then it is also my job to show them love, through kindness, should they come back to me."

Thus the newcomers were left to their own devices on the side of a lake which never had and never would contain fish. But it was a lesson they would have to learn through the long and tedious experience of throwing their lines into the water and waiting for nonexistent fish. For some, it is the only way to learn.

But one truth would remain, as each of the fishermen came and went:

There were no fish in that lake.

This parable is full of lessons that pertain to many aspects of our spiritual existence. The old woman in the story is the embodiment of *faith*. She knows her mission, she loves it, and she carries it out faithfully. The young men are filled with *ego* and do not listen, a fact which she *surrenders* to as their free will.

The old woman of the lake acted out of love each and every time she attempted to warn the fishermen. Neither did she have to donate money or work hard to be of service. She simply had to do the right thing, with the right motive. Her motive, through *love* (*charis*), was to help the fishermen by attempting to save them pain, frustration, and wasted time. When they did not heed her warnings, she responded with *forgiveness* and yet another act of service: she prayed for them.

The old woman felt no glee or satisfaction when the fishermen ended up as she knew they would, with rashes on their legs and hooks in their fingers. She simply carried out her task to heal them. Ultimately she showed love in several ways: love for God, love for her human brethren, love of service, love infused with a kind charity. *Agape*, *philia*, *eunoia*, *charis*.

But the parable of the fish in the lake presents another important teaching, and that is:

> *You cannot save another person from his or her spiritual lessons,*
> *no matter how much you may want to or how hard you try.*

Have you ever tried to warn somebody because you truly didn't want them to be injured—only to watch them ignore you and get hurt anyway? It happens all the time. Do you say, "I told you so?" This parable charges us to have a different response. The old woman in this story does not relish the pain of these men. Instead she waits patiently to pick them up when they fall and help them to heal from both their physical and emotional wounds. This is an unconditional love, which is the goal to which we should all aspire.

For in the same way that we have seen that *no one can steal your destiny*, it is also true that *you cannot force others to achieve their own destiny*. You can merely provide gentle guidance and allow them to make their own choices.

Exercise: **Responding with Love and Support**

- Think of a time when you tried to warn someone about something and they did not listen to you, a time when you were itching to say "I told you so"—and maybe did.
- Was there a different way that you could have approached the situation? Were you loving and gentle, there to pick them up when they fell, or did you find satisfaction in gloating that you were right and they were wrong?
- If you could relive that circumstance, what would you do differently? Can you apply the lessons of unconditional love—or the charge to *love more*—to this scenario?

THE TRUTH ABOUT SOUL MATES

Many people turn to God and pray because they are alone and they want to attract their soul mate. They are in search of romantic and passionate love, *eros*, which is something that God wishes for all of us. There is an old Celtic adage that says, "When God makes them, he

matches them." There is a perfect mate for everyone out there somewhere, and when we are ready, that mate will appear in our lives.

If you are in search of that partner and have not yet found him or
her, take heart. Using this prayer process on a regular basis will naturally attract that person into your life. You really don't have to do anything else to make it happen. See, here is the real, simple soul mate
secret:

> *When you are living in harmony with your mission*
> *You will naturally attract the other souls*
> *Who agreed to fulfill this destiny with you;*
> *These are your true soul mates.*

Remember in the chapter about petal three, service, when we
learned that many people make the same promise and have the same
destiny? Here is the beautiful by-product of that understanding: many
of those who have made promises similar to yours are destined to join
you and work with you toward the same spiritual goals. I refer to these
people as your "family of spirit." In that regard, you have many "soul
mates," and once you connect to this special spirit community, you will
never know a day of loneliness. And the more harmonious you become
with God and your own purpose here on earth, the faster you will draw
those people into your life. They are waiting for you to remember your
promise so that they can show up and help you fulfill it. You are all in
this together!

Is there one "special" soul mate in this family? Yes, there is. And
often that person is out there waiting for you to get spiritually organized so that he or she can show up in your life. Remember that like
attracts like. If you are in an unfortunate place in your life, mentally,
emotionally, or spiritually, you will most often meet and associate with

others who have the same challenges. Conversely, when you are spiritually strong, you will draw healthy new relationships to you. Your fully realized self will attract his or her fully realized self.

The piece of early Christian wisdom that inspires me above most others comes from the Gospel of Philip; it addresses this idea that we were born to live within spiritual families who come from the same divine origins as we do, and the union with these souls is our greatest opportunity for bliss (emphasis mine):

> *There exists forms of union*
> *Higher than any that can be spoken*
> *Stronger than the greatest forces*
> *With the power that is their destiny*
> *Those who live this are no longer separated*
> *They are one.*
> *Is it not necessary for those who know this to recognize each other?*
> *Yet some do not, and they are deprived of this joy.*
> Those who recognize each other
> Know the joy of living together in this fullness.

If you are in search of your perfect mate as well as the rest of your "family of spirit," use this affirmation:

Every day that I work toward fulfilling my life's purpose and my promise to God, I am attracting more and more love into my life.

It is important to note that our lives have finite space for relationships, so if you are following the prayer practice faithfully and are still having trouble attracting your true mate into your life, it could be because you are still holding on to a relationship that is not serving your highest good. Imagine a room that has finite space and a closed door. When there are too many people in the room, someone has to leave to allow someone new to come in.

Exercise: **For Those Looking for Love**

If you are seeking your mate and having trouble finding him or her, you need to ask yourself some important questions:

- Am I holding on to a relationship, or to an idea of love, that has not made me happy, or one that has been unhealthy in any way?
- What have I learned about myself in this relationship? What did I love about it? What did I find unfulfilling or hurtful in it? What has it taught me about what I really need to be happy in a relationship? What was the ultimate lesson of the relationship?

Sometimes painful relationships are part of your spiritual preparation. There is no such thing as wasted time; you may have needed to work out all your lessons in these old relationships so that you don't have to deal with any of that when your true mate arrives. You can jump right in to being happy and fulfilled together! But in order to do that, you must take the lessons with you and assimilate them—and then let go of your former partners. Ask yourself:

- Am I ready to let go, and to release with love, relationships that are not or were not supportive of my emotional and spiritual health? Try this affirmation if it is applicable for you:

Today I release, with love, all those relationships that have hurt me. I bless the lessons and the experience and send gratitude to those who helped me to learn in preparation for attracting my highest love.

ALL LOVE BEGINS WITH YOURSELF

More than anything else, on your path to attracting healthy and joyous relationships into your life, remember this:

Love attracts love.

Act from your highest place, strive to *love more* in everything you do, show your love of God daily in your prayer practice, and your abundance will overflow. And finally, do not forget this one, powerful commandment that is nestled within the others:

Love yourself.

Remember that highest commandment that Jesus entrusted us with: you should love your neighbor as yourself. In other words, you must first love yourself. Self-love is a commandment! And why wouldn't it be? You are precious in God's sight. Never forget that. Because I can assure you that he never forgets that.

XII

Final Thoughts: What Would Jesus Do?

*T*he *city of* Los Angeles is massively diverse in its urban sprawl. My hometown is a melting pot of humanity, rich and alive with cultures and creeds. I was recently physically confronted in the Southern California streets by a particularly virulent man, preaching his political and social agenda. He used hate speech, racist and violent rhetoric, all the while emphasizing that he was a Christian. I noticed that he wore a bracelet embroidered with the letters WWJD, the same bracelet I gave to my children.

What Would Jesus Do?

Had I thought, even for a moment, that I could have had a legitimate conversation with the man about this idea, I would have questioned him: what *would* Jesus do? Yet I know that he would have had an answer that worked for him, one that supported his personal and political agenda, and that he would manage to weave it around the idea of Jesus. His Jesus. Because I realized then that my Jesus, my loving and compassionate master teacher, and the version of Jesus as worshipped by the hate-inciting man on the corner are not the same being.

What *his* Jesus would do and what *my* Jesus would do were two very different things.

I was disturbed for days afterward, as I often am when I contemplate this idea. There are millions of Americans who invoke Jesus every day, myself included. But are we referring to the same Jesus? Does my Jesus look like his Jesus? Does he look like your Jesus? Does he need to?

When I appeared on a nationally broadcast conservative talk show, one of the anchors attacked me after cutting to commercial, saying that I was a "bad Christian." Despite the fact that I pray every day and read scripture regularly, and attempt to share the teachings of Jesus as often as I can, he thought I was a "bad Christian." Why? Because my version of Jesus didn't look like his version.

Which leads to this important question: Who gets to define what the real Jesus looks like? Who determines what the real Jesus would do? Who decides what makes me or anyone else a bad Christian or a good Christian?

And there is only one answer: God. God is the only judge of hearts and minds. The rest of us need to love each other and respect the differences that we hold in peace—for that is what I believe Jesus means when he tells us to love our neighbor. The fact that we all have a love for God and seek to serve him should unite us, not divide us.

Within the pages of this book, I have introduced you to the Jesus I know, through his words and his work and the miracles they have wrought in my life. It is up to you to decide in your heart and soul what your Jesus looks like. I do not seek to convert or proselytize; I simply seek to share. The rest is between you and God.

The Gospel of Philip says that *Christ contains all: man, angel, mystery, Father.* Philip tells us that *Jesus does not reveal himself as he is, but according to the capacity of those who want to see him: to the great he ap-*

pears great, to the small he appears small, to the human he appears as a man, to the angels as an angel.

I have quoted from a number of sources as examples and for inspiration within this book. I most often use the words of Jesus and try to quote him directly whenever I can. While I refer to multiple translations, including the literal Greek text, the majority of quotes in this book are from the New International Version. My personal constant, and the source that I recognize as supremely authoritative, is the Gospel of Matthew. When I question anything in the teachings of Jesus, I refer to Matthew before any other source; that gospel is my foundation. While studying the New Testament in depth over the years, I came to a personal conclusion that the Gospel of Matthew resonated the most with me, followed closely by the service-oriented Gospel of Luke.

To supplement Matthew, I refer to other early Christian sources, most frequently the Gnostic Gospels of Philip, Thomas, and Mary Magdalene. I am inspired by these writings of the very faithful early followers of Christ, and my own understanding of Jesus has been dramatically enhanced by reading the Gnostic material. These later gospels show us how Christianity survived as a living tradition outside Rome, removed from the political influences of the early church. I therefore find them as fascinating as they are illuminating, but I should point out that not all Christians feel the same way about this material. The same conservative talk show host who called me a bad Christian also pointed to my use of the Gnostic material as one of the factors in his judgment against me. Many traditional Christians who prefer literal interpretations of the Bible refuse to acknowledge the Gnostic material. Some say it is heretical.

As I wrote this book, I came to realize that the conservative talk show host and the man screaming on the street may not share my point of view on the Gnostic Gospels or much else, but I am willing to bet that we all have one thing in common: we all know the Lord's Prayer. If you put the three of us in a room together, this is the common ground we could find. And so I hold on to the belief that this perfect, beautiful prayer can unite all of us in loving God and loving each other.

Finally, inspired by my own excitement over the freshly discovered gospels that continue to come to light, I will leave you with the final words of Jesus as they are found in the Gnostic Gospel of Judas:

> *Look, you have been told everything.*
> *Lift up your eyes and look at the cloud and the light within it*
> *and the stars surrounding it.*
> *The star that leads the way*
> *is your star.*

I pray that you will follow your star and generate the miracles that will lead you, and all of us, on the path of creating heaven on earth.

Appendixes

WHICH VERSION OF THE LORD'S PRAYER DO YOU PREFER?

Important note: You will find that any version of the Lord's Prayer you choose to use is entirely compatible with the practices within this book. Please feel free to recite the version that you are most comfortable with!

While writing this book, I was faced with the difficult task of deciding which translation of the Lord's Prayer to use. The Lord's Prayer is an important aspect of spiritual identity for many Christians, some of whom are disconcerted by even a single changed word. I once lived in a culture where the way a citizen recited the Lord's Prayer labeled them very specifically and could even be a matter of life or death. As such, I am very sensitive to the issue of "version."

In the final analysis, I did not choose to use the version I grew up with and am most personally comfortable with. I chose the one that I believe best represents, in English, the words Jesus spoke. In my biblical studies, when there is a choice to be made, I go directly to Jesus' own words.

Many Evangelical Christians will recognize this version. It is nearly identical to their own, with a single exception: the final word. Within the original prayer, Jesus says in the literal translation, *deliver us from evil*. In later versions this was changed to read *deliver us from the evil one*. I have again used the original texts as my reference for this, as it is the one element of translation that affects the meaning of the prayer and its practice. Evil, as defined here in chapter 10, represents that which separates us from God. There are numerous versions of evil, not a single "one."

I was raised with the version used most frequently in both the Episcopal and Catholic traditions, which has substituted the word *trespasses* for *debts* since the third century.

> *Our Father who art in heaven,*
> *hallowed be thy name.*
> *Thy kingdom come.*
> *Thy will be done on earth, as it is in heaven.*
> *Give us this day our daily bread,*
> *and forgive us our trespasses,*
> *as we forgive those who trespass against us,*
> *and lead us not into temptation,*
> *but deliver us from evil.*

The word *trespasses* was likely substituted for *debts* to differentiate between material debts and spiritual offenses. The Greek word used in the original gospel translates as something more than financial debt; it represents "sinning against another" rather than "owing money." Other versions of the prayer substitute the word *sins* for *debts*, which may come from the original Aramaic, the language in which Jesus first spoke the prayer. In Aramaic, the words *sin* and *debt* are interchangeable. Non-Christian groups who use the prayer, for example the United

Church of Religious Science as well as some twelve-step recovery programs, substitute the word *errors* for *debts*.

Many Christians recite an ending phrase to the prayer, called a doxology:

For thine is the kingdom and the power and the glory forever.

The word *doxology* comes from two Greek roots: *doxa*, which means "glory," and *logos*, which refers to "words." Thus a doxology contains words of glory or praise to God. In the case of the Lord's Prayer, it is a beautiful and powerful supplement to the original words Jesus gave to us, but as it does not appear in the earliest form of the Gospel of Matthew, I have not used it within the practice. The doxology at the end of the Lord's Prayer first appears in a manuscript from the late first century called the Didache, or the Teachings of the Apostles. In later versions of the Gospel of Matthew, from the late fifth century on, the doxology is added to the prayer.

If the doxology is part of your daily practice, so much the better. You can never give God too many words of praise!

The differences that make up the versions of the Lord's Prayer are minor in terms of what Jesus set out to teach us. I do not believe that God, the unlimited divine mind and source of all love, would really care whether you said "Our father *which* art in heaven" or "Our father *who* art in heaven." For the purposes of the practice in this book, none of these differences matter.

The two billion of us who revere these words and use this prayer regularly are ultimately more alike than we are different. We are all the children of Our Father.

INSPIRATIONAL PRAYERS TO
SUPPLEMENT YOUR PRACTICE

Within the pages of this book I referred to prayers that inspire me, specifically those authored by Saint Teresa of Ávila and Saint Francis of Assisi. These are regular additions to my own prayer practice, and I offer them to you here that they may inspire your own.

From Saint Francis of Assisi comes this, which is part of my own daily ritual:

> *Lord, make me an instrument of Thy peace;*
> *where there is hatred, let me sow love;*
> *where there is injury, pardon;*
> *where there is doubt, faith;*
> *where there is despair, hope;*
> *where there is darkness, light;*
> *and where there is sadness, joy.*
>
> *O Divine Master,*
> *grant that I may not so much seek to be consoled as to console;*

to be understood, as to understand;
to be loved, as to love;
for it is in giving that we receive,
it is in pardoning that we are pardoned,
and it is in dying that we are born to eternal life.

From Saint Teresa of Ávila come these:

May today I find peace within.
May I trust my highest power
that I am exactly where I am meant to be.
May I not forget the infinite possibilities
that are born of faith.
May I use those gifts that I have received,
and pass on the love that has been given to me.
May I be content knowing I am a child of God.
May this presence settle into my bones,
and allow my soul the freedom to sing, dance, praise, and love.

Let nothing upset you,
let nothing startle you.
All things pass;
Yet God does not change.
Patience wins all that it seeks.
Whoever has God
lacks nothing:
God alone is enough

During Shane's illness, we were presented with a prayer to the first century apostle Saint Jude. We utilized this prayer each day in conjunction with our Catholic friends who were committed to the use of this prayer during times of crisis. The Saint Jude prayer became very important to us as a family, and we promised at that time to share it with the world when the time was right.

Blessed apostle, St. Jude, you were a faithful servant and friend of Jesus
And people honor and invoke you universally.
Please help to bring me visible and speedy assistance.
Comfort me in this great need that I may receive the consolation and help of heaven
in all my necessities, tribulations, and sufferings, particularly [state your request].
I will praise God with you always and I promise to be ever mindful of this great favor
to always honor you as my special and powerful patron
and to gratefully encourage devotion to you.

Acknowledgments

The same week that I completed this manuscript, UCLA held a reunion for all the babies and families who had been saved through their NICU. It was a celebration of life and miracles, and a reminder of just how harmonious faith and science can be together. I talked with other parents that day, some wearing T-shirts that said "My child is a miracle." They all had astonishing, inspirational stories to tell, and all of them would credit prayer as instrumental to those miracles. These stories remind us that miracles are a daily occurrence. They are there for the taking, for everyone who puts his or her faith into action.

This reunion was an example of so many of the things that I have written about in the preceding pages. Every one of these people— nurses, respiratory therapists, doctors, social workers—are examples of service. They save lives every day, and not just the lives of the infants in their care; they save the parents as well with their compassionate understanding.

I realized, as I watched all the "miracle children" playing with their medical caregivers, just how much the wonderful people at UCLA have become a part of our family history and the fabric of our lives, and I would like to recognize them with appreciation for all that they do: Joyce, Leslie, Dr. Mir, Dr. Smith, Mary Ann, Mary V., Magdalena

(Maggie), Jodi, Anahit, Barbara, Michael, Bess, Tracy, and finally Nancy Hansen, who worked with Shane for almost two years as part of the study and was so instrumental to his development.

Stacey Kishi is part of this book and part of my journey. She was with me on that fateful day in Chartres when we both knew that we would never be quite the same again, and on many days since. Among other blessings, she encouraged me to continue on the complex quest to understand the labyrinth and all that it offers us.

Love and thanks to Maureen Breen in Chicago for allowing us to share in the miracle of baby Patrick Joseph, whose story echoes Shane's in so many ways and reinforced my own belief system with such strength; you can read more about little Patrick, and other miracles, on my website.

I am grateful for everyone on the Magdalene Line Forum who have included me in their stories of the miraculous: you all inspire me so often. Keep creating those miracles!

To Sarah Symons, John Berger, and Becky Bavinger of the Emancipation Network and Made by Survivors, I give my gratitude, respect, and love for all that they do each day to help improve the lives of women and children who have been rescued from slavery. Their work inspires me daily to go to greater lengths in my own commitments to service as we continue to cocreate programs that will ensure security and happiness for survivors. Please visit www.MadebySurvivors.com to see how you can fulfill your own service commitments.

Special thanks to the stunning and talented Dana Tynan, who has been teaching me about the miracle of unconditional friendship since the fourth grade; as always to Patrick Ruffino, my spiritual twin brother; and Dawn Molkenbur, for her continued love and generous support of my work and family; and to Filip Coppens, for proving these theories perfectly and helping with the final edits.

I am blessed to have learned from so many wise teachers who have preserved this wisdom—in stone, glass, on paper, and through oral traditions—over so many centuries. There are too many to name, while some are unknown, and others cannot be named. But each has left a legacy in the name of love.

I am indebted to the work of Richmond Lattimore and his literal translation from the Greek of the New Testament, as it opened my eyes to so much. I am also a fan of the Archaeological Study Bible, which contains the New International Version, and recommend it for students of scripture who want to study on their own. Further, the Gnostic Gospels and early Christian writings hold so much wisdom, and I would encourage the spiritual seeker to explore them. I am most fond of, and use regularly, the translations of the gospels of Philip, Thomas, and Mary by the esteemed French theologian Jean-Yves LeLoup and have used them throughout this book. A wonderful website, www.Early ChristianWritings.com, provides a directory and free online translations of hundreds of manuscripts. It also has links to early Hebrew writings and to a large number of online books.

This book would not have happened without the support of my archangelic agent, Larry Kirshbaum, and my brilliant editor, Trish Todd, and I thank them for supporting me in my work. They are two of the miracles in my life.

The miracle of my family is the greatest of them all. They are the source of my joy; they are my abundance.

As a special gift to my readers, you can visit my website at www.kathleenmcgowan.com, to download an inspirational version of the Lord's Prayer set to music by Peter McGowan. Lyrics by Jesus.

And I couldn't end this book without expressing my gratitude to God, who is all good all the time.